UNIVERSITY OF NORTH CAROLINA
STUDIES IN THE ROMANCE LANGUAGES AND LITERATURES
Number 100

THE FOUR INTERPOLATED STORIES IN THE
ROMAN COMIQUE:
THEIR SOURCES AND UNIFYING FUNCTION

THE FOUR INTERPOLATED STORIES IN THE *ROMAN COMIQUE:*

THEIR SOURCES AND UNIFYING FUNCTION

BY

FREDERICK ALFRED DE ARMAS

CHAPEL HILL

THE UNIVERSITY OF NORTH CAROLINA PRESS

DEPÓSITO LEGAL: V. 1.406 - 1971

ARTES GRÁFICAS SOLER, S. A. - JÁVEA, 28 - VALENCIA (8) - 1971

PREFACE

Paul Scarron's *Roman comique* (1651) has been considered by most critics as a work devoid of organization. Paul Morillot refers to "le désordre impertinent de l'intrigue," while André le Breton states that Scarron's novel, written without a preconceived plan, is part of la Fronde littéraire," in opposition to the school of Honoré d'Urfée in which he even includes the *Histoire comique* of Cyrano de Bergerac.

This attitude is reflected in critics' consideration of the four interpolated *nouvelles* included in the *Roman comique*. They are viewed as concessions to the romanesque taste of the times, and having no relation to the action of the story. In the present comparison of the Spanish originals to the French version by Scarron, I will attempt to demonstrate how the author of the *Roman comique* changed his stories in order to mirror the action of the novel. The *récits* of Destin and La Caverne will also reflect this purpose. These *récits*, which trace the early lives of the main characters of the novel, and which are also considered extraneous by critics, will be grouped in this study with the *nouvelles*. An analysis of the composition of the novel stemming from these interpolations, which should be the prime consideration since they represent more than half of the novel, will show that the *Roman comique* is not without a plan but has a definite structure which serves the action.

It is with considerable gratitude that I take the opportunity to thank Professor George B. Daniel of the University of North Carolina Department of Romance Languages for his interest and patience in directing the preparation of this study as a doctoral dissertation. I should also like to thank the administrators of the Smith Fund for enabling me to acquire microfilm copies of a number of indispensable and otherwise unobtainable works, and the Research Council of Louisiana State University, Baton Rouge, for their financial support.

TABLE OF CONTENTS

	Page
PREFACE	7
CHAPTER I.—INTRODUCTION: A Brief history of the short narrative in France up to the time of the "Roman Comique"	11
— II.—"L'Amante invisible"	28
— III.—"A trompeur, trompeur et demi"	51
— IV.—"Le juge de sa propre cause"	78
— V.—"Les deux frères rivaux"	110
CONCLUSION	144
BIBLIOGRAPHY	146

CHAPTER I

INTRODUCTION: A BRIEF HISTORY OF THE SHORT NARRATIVE IN FRANCE UP TO THE TIME OF THE *ROMAN COMIQUE*

The first collection of short stories in France was written sometime between 1450 and 1460. It is the Cent *nouvelles nouvelles,* sometimes attributed to Antoine de La Salle. However, it is with the sixteenth century that these collections of short prose fiction become popular. This type of fiction is derived from two sources. First, the French short fiction of the Middle Ages, mostly anecdotal and general, and in the case of the *fabliaux,* not even in prose. This first type includes the *contes dévots,* apologues, *exempla* and fables. The second source is the Italian *novelle,* which achieved its peak with Bocaccio's *Decameron* (1353). Other Italian authors who were influential during the sixteenth century are Sercambi, Sermini, Masuccio, and Morlini.

It is difficult at times to separate the native and the Italian sources, since both often are anecdotal, general, very short, and meant for either amusement or very specific instruction. The most important authors of this developing art include as early representatives Philippe de Vigneulles and Nicolas de Troyes. The latter wrote *Le Grand paragon des nouvelles nouvelles* (1537). This is a typical work of the period because it combines Italian sources with the traditional ones. A brief analysis of "D'une Fille qui fit aller trois compagnons, amoureux d'elle, coucher en un cimetière" demonstrates clearly these characteristics. In this story a young girl attempts to rid herself of three *galants.* She devises a scheme of having each go to the cemetery in order to placate the spirit of her dead mother. The first is to go and sit on her mother's grave until midnight, covered by a white cloth. The second is to dress up as a policeman and go an hour later, while the third is to be dressed as a devil. She will reward them only if they can stay till midnight. The conclusion of the story is obvious: each sees the other, is frightened, and does not remain in the cemetary until midnight. She is thus rid of them.

As can be seen, the story is only an anecdote. Its purpose is to amuse, and the structure has no complexities. Its humor has no subtlety. As for the characters, they have no individuality, but are only general figures. For example, the girl is not even given a name but is referred to as "une jeune fille sage et honnête et de bonnes mœurs." [1]

Bonaventure Despériers is another well known *conteur* of the sixteenth century. In 1558 his *Les Nouvelles Recreations et joyeux devis* appeared, fourteen years after his death. Reproduced here is one of his typical stories, "Comparaison des Alquemistes à la bonne femme qui portait une pottée de lait au marché":

> Chacun sait que le commun langage des Alquemistes, c'est qu'ils se promettent un monde de richesses, et qu'ils savent des secrets de nature que tous les hommes ensemble ne savent pas: mais à la fin tout leur cas s'en va en fumée, tellement que leur alquemis se pourrait plus proprement dire: Art qui mine, ou Art qui n'est mie: et ne les saurait-on mieux comparer qu'à une bonne femme qui portait une potée de lait au marché, faisant son compte ainsi: qu'elle la vendrait deux liards; de ces deux liards elle en achèterait une douzaine d'œufs, lesquels elle mettrait couver, et en aurait une douzaine de poussins; ces poussins deviendraient grands; ces chapons vaudraient cinq sols la pièce; ce serait un écu et plus, dont elle achèterait deux cochons, mâle et femelle, qui deviendraient grands et en feraient une douzaine d'autres, qu'elle vendrait vingt sols la pièce après les avoir nourris quelque temps: ce seraient douze francs, dont elle achèterait une jument qui porterait un beau poulain, lequel croîtrait et deviendrait tant gentil: il sauterait et ferait *hin*. Et, en disant *hin,* la bonne femme de l'aise

---

[1] Jules Hasselmann, ed., *Les Conteurs français du XVIe siècle* (Paris: Librairie Larousse, 1945). Throughout this work, all diacritical markings are as found in the original.

qu'elle avait en son compte, se prit à faire la ruade que ferait son poulain, e, en la faisant, sa potée de lait va tomber et se répandit toute. Et voilà ses œufs, ses poussins, ses chapons, ses cochons, sa jument, et son poulain, tous par terre. Ainsi les Alquemistes, après qu'ils ont bien fournayé, charbonné, luté, soufflé, distillé, calciné, congelé, fixé, liquefié, vitriefié, putrefié, il ne faut que casser un alambic pour les mettre au compte de la bonne femme. [2]

All the main characteristics of the sixteenth century story can be noted in this selection. It is an anecdote and very short. There is no sophistication of structure, since the author is not interested in how he tells the story, but rather what he tells. There are no individualistic characters, only general ones: a woman, an alchemist. In the comparison, a moral is indicated. Thus, in addition to being amused by a clever comparison, the story is designed with a moral in mind so as to instruct the reader. Consequently, it is derived from the tradition of the *exempla,* while the previous one is more akin to the satiric tales in the manner of Rabelais.

Yet, this very coarse narrative will have a great influence. First, it is Despériers' preliminary handling of the alchemist as the man who is out of touch with reality. He will again pick up this image and develop it much further in his *Cymbalum Mundi.* Here, Mercury laughs at alchemists who are searching for remnants of the philosopher's stone which he reputedly had brought to earth and scattered in a specific place.

Cymbalum Mundi has sometimes been considered as a source for Cervantes' "Coloquio de los perros." If true, it would certainly be interesting to realize that the Spanish author of the *Novelas ejemplares* was acquainted with one of the foremost French *conteurs* of the sixteenth century. However, other than the fact that the dogs can speak in both works, there is no other resemblance, if not the fact that Cervantes mentions an alchemist in his work.

The "Comparaison des Alquemistes à la bonne femme qui portait une pottée de lait au marché" is also the source for La Fontaine's "La Laitière et le pot au lait." La Fontaine is the only major seventeenth century author of short stories that was influenced by the Italian and the medieval tradition.

---

[2] *Ibid.,* pp. 37-38.

Some other important collections of tales in the sixteenth century are: *Les Propos rustiques* (1547) and *Les Contes et discours d'Eutrapel* (1585) by Noel du Fail, mainly rustic tales; Henri Estienne's *Apologie pour Hérodote,* mainly satires on the church; Jacques Yver's *Printemps*; Guillaume des Autels *Mythistoire barragouine de Fanfreluche et Gaudichon* (1574); Philippe d'Alcripe's *Nouvelle fabrique des excellents traits de verite* (1579); and Benigne Poissenot's *L'Eté* (1583).

A final example from the latter part of the century, "Les Suisses et le boiteux," a tale found in *Les Serées* (1584) by Guillaume Bouchet indicates that the short story developed very little beyond the general, anecdotal style. The structure and plot of the story is just as simple as any of the earlier ones. Four men on horseback pass by Blois, where the king happens to be. One of the men falls off his horse, and the Swiss guards come to help him. Thinking that he has a broken leg, the guards try to mend it; but this person was already lame before falling from his horse, and does not need assistance.

The rest of the tale tells how this misunderstanding, caused by people who did not speak the same language, was finally resolved. As can be seen, this is no more than an anecdote. Characters are still general: the lame man, the guards, the King. No individualization can be detected. The story is very short and there is no complication in the plot. This tale was probably derived from oral tradition.

There is, however, one work written in France in 1559 that shows more sophistication than any of these other tales. It is the *Heptaméron* by Marguerite de Navarre. The setting is very similar to Boccaccio's *Decameron,* a work that had been translated into the French by Antoine Le Maçon in 1545. A group of bathers from Cauterets retires to Notre-Dame de Serrance in the Pyrenees because of a flood. There, they tell tales for amusement. These tales, although more sophisticated and generally lengthier than other collections of *contes* in this century, are still very much in the same tradition. Some can be considered as *exempla* on what true love should be like, following her attitudes on the *querelle de la femme,* and her interest in Plato, as explained by Ficcino. Other tales resemble what Jules Hasselman considers to be the dominant trend of the sixteenth century short story:

> L'esprit gaulois, réaliste, railleur et licencieux, qui avait parodié avec Rabelais la légende merveilleuse, domine l'inspiration des conteurs du XVIe siècle.[3]

These tales are still told in chronological order, having a very simple structure. Many of the characters are still not individuals, and the plot is often simple. Some of the stories are just anecdotes. They are still in the tradition of the *conte*, having just one line of action which is taken to its conclusion without any embellishments or complexities.

Instead, then, of developing, the *conte*, derived from medieval and Italian sources, remained static. *Exempla* and humorous incidents were told in anecdotal form. In addition, after the middle of the sixteenth century, there was in France a reaction against anything Italian. G. Hainsworth discusses the result in a work that must be considered essential to any study of the short story in France during the seventeenth century, *Les "Novelas Ejemplares" de Cervantes en France au XVIIe siècle*:

> A partir de 1555, il y eut, comme on le sait, une forte réaction contre l'influence italienne. Vers la fin du siècle, le genre se trouve à peu près dans un état de stagnation, et l'on constate même un déclin considérable dans le nombre de nouvelles produites en France. Quand on en reprendra la publication au début du siècle suivant, ce ne sera plus, croyons-nous, sous l'égide de l'Italie; et Marchesi, dans son ouvrage par ailleurs plein d'intérêt et d'érudition, se trompe certainement en affirmant que la nouvelle française du XVIIe siècle, loin de marquer une inspiration espagnole, se tient toujours à la tradition de la *novella*. On s'explique pourtant très bien l'erreur de Marchesi. C'est que, pour lui, la nouvelle du XVIIe siècle, ce n'est pas celle de Sorel ou de Segrais mais celle de *Verboquet le généreux*, de Louis Garon, du sieur de Favoral, et de d'Ouville. A ne considérer que les ouvrages de ce genre-ci, on est certainement porté à croire que la *novella* conserve tout son prestige au XVIIe siècle. Destinés exclusivement à faire rire, ces recueils de bons mots, d'anecdotes presque toujours courtes, trahissent, et même trop clairement, leur provenance italienne. Ils

---

[3] *Ibid.*, p. 6.

constituent d'ailleurs toute une branche de la littérature de cette époque.[4]

Thus, throughout the seventeenth century, this branch of literature, which we call anecdotal, continued to exist; however, it did not develop. A second branch, the *histoire tragique,* derived from the tales of Bandello and some of the sixteenth century authors like J. Yver and Poissenot, also played a very minor role, since the only worthy imitators it had in France were Rosset, who in 1614 published the *Histoires tragiques,* and Jean Pierre Camus, the author of religious novels, who also wrote some shorter tales. G. Hainsworth discusses several authors that continued this tradition and concludes:

> Quant à ces derniers, si l'*histoire tragique* perdait entre leurs mains tout l'intérêt littéraire qu'elle eut du temps de Bandello, c'est que, grâce à l'évidente popularité des sujets lugubres (comparable à celles des sujets scabreux dont témoignent tant de recueils de contes), ils ont pu, pour la plupart, enfanter machinalement, et sans la moindre préoccupation artistique des ouvrages dont le succès était presque assuré d'avance. L'*histoire tragique* a subi ainsi une dégénération très analogue à celle du conte facétieux, et quoique plus intéressante, en sa matière, que le conte, elle ne pouvait guère contribuer, dans l'état où nous la trouvons vers le milieu du siècle, à l'évolution de la nouvelle française.[5]

The general form of the short story was certainly in a state of flux, even decline, at the beginnnig of the seventeenth century. A new form was necessary. Less than two years after their publication in Spain, there appeared in France the first translation of Miguel de Cervantes' *Novelas ejemplares.* Six were translated by François de Rosset and the other six, by Vital d'Audiguier. This represents the beginning in both France and Spain of a new form of short story which will become extremely popular throughout the century. Cervantes himself was aware of his originality:

---

[4] G. Hainsworth, *Les "Novelas Ejemplares" de Cervantes en France au XVIIe siècle* (Paris: Librairie Ancienne Honoré Champion, 1933), p. 102.

[5] *Ibid.,* p. 109.

INTRODUCTION: A BRIEF HISTORY OF THE SHORT NARRATIVE... 17

> Y es así, que yo soy el primero que he novelado en lengua castellana; que las muchas novelas que en ella andan impresas, todas son traducidas de lenguas extranjeras, y estas son mías propias, no imitadas ni hurtadas: mi ingenio las engendró y las parió mi pluma y van creciendo en los brazos de la estampa.[6]

The situation of the short story in Spain prior to Cervantes' publication was very similar to that in France. Authors would either imitate the literature of *exempla* as written by don Juan Manuel, who was following the same tradition of *El libro de los engaños,* and *Calila e Dimna,* translated from the Arabic but of Indian origin; or borrowed from the Italian *novelle.*[7]

In addition to the two types mentioned above, the Italian *novelle* also includes stories derived from the *exempla,* or the *fabliaux* which, since they are already a part of the medieval tradition, are not treated separately. There is, however, a fourth type of *novelle,* as pointed out by G. Hainsworth:

> Nous songeons aux lecteurs fort nombreux qui n'ont vu dans la *novella* qu'un court récit amusant, même indécent, une sorte de fabliau en prose. Sous l'hypnotisme de cet aspect du genre italien, la critique moderne a même pu oublier en un moment de distraction, que ce genre en a un autre tout à fait différent.... Les diverses fortunes de deux amants, séparés pour être réunis à la fin, avec les reconnaissances providentielles d'enfants estimés perdus, et autres éléments du roman grec.[8]

This last type has not been discussed, since it had little influence in the short story in France during the sixteenth century. With Cervantes' assertion that he is not imitating anyone in his *novelas* the fourth of Italian *novella* must be differentiated from the new Spanish *novela.*

Juan de Timoneda, an early Spanish imitator of the Italian *novellas* uses, among others, this fourth type. An example of this is

---

[6] Miguel de Cervantes, *Novelas ejemplares* (Buenos Aires: Editorial Sopena Argentina S. A., 1962), I, 7.

[7] An excellent discussion of the early short fiction can be found in M. Menéndez Pelayo's *Orígenes de la novela* (Madrid: 1907), II.

[8] Hainsworth, *op. cit.,* p. 24.

found in the first "patraña" from his work *El patrañuelo* (1567). An analyses of this story will show its close affinity to the other Italian types, and not to the *novela* of Cervantes. Two children are born on the same day to two rich merchants from Alexandria. Furthermore, the children are identical. The merchants get together and have Pantana raise them both. She is the only one who knows how to tell them apart. When they grow up, Pantana gives each merchant the son of the other. One of these young men falls in love with whom he thinks is his own sister, Argentina, and has a child by her. The father leaves the child in the forest when he discovers it, and orders Argentine to marry the other Tolomeo (they also had identical names), who is actually her brother. A saintly monk in the end turns out to be Pantana, and the child substitution is explained. The child whom the merchant had left in the woods ha been discovered and raised by Pantana.

This very intricate plot is narrated in four pages. None of the characters are individuals, but are merely general types. The story is told in chronological order, having no suspense or sophistication of structure. It is filled with events that are completely *invraisemblable*. The substitution of children and final recognition show the Greek origin of the tale, since it points to the methods used by Heliodorus in the *Aethiopica,* a work first published in Europe which became very popular throughout the continent, being translated into many languages including Italian (1556) and Spanish (1587). Thus, although the plot points to something more than an anecdote, the basic form remains the same. The only interest is found in the basic intrigue, although there is not even any suspense.

The Italian *novelle* and their early Spanish imitations as found in *El patrañuelo* are very different from Cervantes' *novela*. Hainsworth, discussing, in general, the differences between the Italian and the Spanish short stories, points out that in length, chastity, and seriousness, they are totally different. He also points out that presentation becomes more important than subject matter in the Spanish tale. The plot per se is not the only element of interest, since this structure is created to provide surprise and to point to the action of the tale. G. Hainsworth points in his comparison:

> Alors que Boccace commence presque toujours par nommer les héros de son récit, et l'endroit où se passe son

action, procédant ensuite à développer, pas à pas, la série des événements, Cervantès plonge souvent *in medias res,* et tâche par divers moyens d'éveiller dès l'abord l'intérêt du lecteur. [9]

Another difference that must be added is the fact that while the Italian or even the story derived from the Middle Ages pays no attention to verisimilitude, the Spanish story is grounded in reality. It does not usually present the unbelievable recognitions or coincidences found in the Greek romances that were imitated by the Italian *novelle.* [10] Instead they deal with very real romantic adventures. Caroline B. Bourland, in her work, *The Short Story in Spain in the Seventeenth Century,* states that the main interest of these *novelas* is the accurate portrayal of the customs of the times. Kidnappings, elopements and duels, although appearing to us very romanesque, were integral parts of life of seventeenth-century Spain.

The delineation of characters is also another difference between the Italian and the Spanish short story. The Spanish authors, not just narrating an anecdote, but making their works rather extensive, have time to present a character that has individual traits. Finally, the plot itself and its handling shows a marked difference from the Italian story that only presents an outline narrative. Caroline Bourland, comparing the Spanish to the Italian short story, states:

> They are marked, generally speaking, by multiplicity of incident and frequent shifting of scene, two features common also to the drama of the period. The plot is likely to be loosely constructed and to be burdened with digressions or extraneous episodes which are very detrimental to the structure of the story, although in many cases interesting to the student of social history for the light they throw upon contemporary conditions. Letters, usually love letters, quoted in *extenso,* are often introduced, as well as verses, which may be texts of serenades or of songs sung in social

---

[9] *Ibid.,* p. 5.
[10] An exception to this is Cervantes' "La Gitanilla" where the influence of the Greek romances is noticeable. (It should be remembered that the author of Dom Quijote would later write a full fledged novel based on the Greek romances: *Persiles y Segismunda*). Yet, a comparison between Timoneda's first "patraña" and Cervantes' "La Gitanilla" will yield all the major differences that exist between the Italian *novelle* and the Spanish *novela* as discussed in this chapter.

gatherings, poems recited for the entertainment of friends or used by lovers as vehicles to express their feelings of joy or of despair. These interpolations, without adding much to the novela, retard its action and greatly extend its length, which is often further increased by the method *à tiroir* employed in their telling. A single story sometimes includes two or three almost independent narratives in which certain of the characters give their life histories up to the time of their appearance upon the scene. These autobiographies not only tend to make the story very long but also to keep the centre of interest shifting from one person to another, and thus to produce an impression of noncoherence in the action greater than exists in reality, since the different threads are usually brought together at the end of the novela and the various personages find the solution of their individual problems in the general denouement. [11]

Basic differences between the Spanish *novela* and the Italian short story include the movement away from the anecdotal and toward the realm of the romanesque. Its beginning *in medias res*, the intricacies of structure, the embellishments and the delineation of character link the *novela* to the novel, although it is somewhat removed from the heroic French novel, an imitation of the romances of chivalry. It is also removed from the Byzantine tale and Greek novel, coming closer to the sentimental novel of the earlier seventeenth century in France.

The Spanish *novela* had an almost immediate influence on the French authors of the period. Soon after the appearance of Cervantes' *Novelas ejemplares*, many Spanish authors began writing this type of short story. French authors immediately translated or imitated them. In 1620, Rosset, one of Cervantes' translators, published the *Histoires graves et sententieuses*, a translation of ten stories of Trancoso. The following year, J. Baudoin published the *Nouvelles morales, en suitte de celles de Cervantes*, a translation of Diego Agreda y Vargas' *Novelas morales*.

In 1623 appeared the *Nouvelles françaises* of Charles Sorel. Although G. Hainsworth finds that these *nouvelles* are in the Spanish

---

[11] Caroline B. Bourland, *The Short Story in Spain in the Seventeenth Century* (Portland, Maine: Southworth Press for Smith College, 1927), pp. 19-20.

tradition, they are mostly original and are not taken from any particular author.[12] This move to produce stories in the Spanish tradition, but without imitating a particular author, was not followed at this time. Instead, adaptations and imitations continued to appear. The most important ones are: *Les Nouvelles de Lancelot tirées des plus célèbres auteurs espagnols* taken from Gonzalo de Céspedes y Meneses and Francisco de Lugo y Dávila; *Les Nouvelles tragicomiques* by Paul Scarron, taken from María de Zayas y Sotomayor and Alonso Gerónimo de Salas Barbadillo; *Les Nouvelles amoureuses et exemplaires,* a translation made by d'Ouville of María de Zayas y Sotomayor; and Vanel's translations at the end of the century of *novelas* by María de Zayas y Sotomayor and Alonso de Castillo Solórzano. However, by 1660, the Spanish *novela* was being transformed into a native French form. As early as 1656, Segrais published the *Nouvelles françaises,* which, although in the Spanish form, are original stories. In the introduction, Segrais promises not to use translations but to create stories as good as the Spanish. In 1658 Ancelin published *L'Amant ressucité,* the first original *nouvelle* to be published singly, and not as part of a collection. Discussing this change that took place around 1660, Dorothy Dallas, speaking of Segrais, states:

> En somme, *Les Nouvelles Françaises* servent de transition entre les romans de dix tomes et les petites fictions qui entourent et rendent possible *La Princesse de Clèves.* [13]

The Spanish *novela* influenced prose fiction to such an extent that it changed its form from the heroic novel to a type very similar to the modern novel and which produced a great masterpiece: *La Princesse de Clèves.* This new type also resembles the sentimental novel of the earlier part of the seventeenth century, and the latter part of the sixteenth. Frederik W. Vogler summarizes the affinity of these two types:

> By indicating works which though imperfect do correspond in many respects to the modern definition of "novel," this

---

[12] Hainsworth, *op. cit.*, pp. 121-138.
[13] Dorothy Frances Dallas, *Le Roman français de 1660 à 1680* (Paris: Librairie Universitaire J. Gamber, 1932), p. 152.

type of research has caused the point of origin of the modern French novel to be shifted in the thinking of most of its students from Madame de La Fayette's work to the sentimental fiction of the late sixteenth century.[14]

The Spanish *novela* should then be studied together with the early sentimental fiction in order to construe the origin of the modern novel in France.

Some Spanish tales were not included in collections or published separately. They were instead used as interpolated stories in novels. As early as the latter part of the sixteenth century, we have examples of this. Montemayor's *La Diana,* the pastoral novel that so much influenced d'Urfé's *Astrée,* contained an interpolated story: "Historia del Abencerrage y de la hermosa Jarifa." Mateo Alemán's picaresque novel, *Guzmán Alfarache* (1599), contains four interpolated stories, one of which was very popular: "Ozmín y Daraja." It was first imitated by N. Lancelot in *La Palme de Fidelité* (1620). The best known, however, are the two interpolated stories found in the first part of *Don Quijote de la Mancha*. One of them, "El Curioso Impertinente," was translated as early as 1608 by Nicolas Baudouin.

Thus, when Paul Scarron decided to include four interpolated stories in his *Roman comique,* he was acting under the prevalent Spanish influence. Three of these stories were taken from Alonso de Castillo Solórzano, the most popular and prolific of all the Spanish short story writers of the seventeenth century. The other was taken from a *novela* by María de Zayas y Sotomayor, a friend of Castillo Solórzano, and possibly the best woman author of *novelas* in Spain during the seventeenth century. The idea to include interpolated *novelas* in his novel was certainly then derived from Spanish novels, although some French works had already adapted this custom. Also, the *novelas* themselves are Spanish. Is there any Spanish influence in Scarron's novel other than the interpolated stories? According to J. Demogeot, there is:

> Le meilleur de ses ouvrages, son *Roman comique,* est aussi la plus heureuse des inspirations qu'il reçut de l'Es-

---

[14] Frederick Wright Vogler, *Vital d'Audiguier and the Early Seventeenth Century French Novel* (Chapel Hill: U. of North Carolina Press, 1964), p. 16.

INTRODUCTION: A BRIEF HISTORY OF THE SHORT NARRATIVE... 23

pagne, s'il est vrai, ce qui semble probable, qu'il en doive l'idée première au *Viage entretenido* de Rojas Villandrado. [15]

Paul Morillot denies this, and all Spanish influence:

> Il est impossible cette fois d'attribuer à l'Espagne l'honneur d'avoir fourni le modèle. On a cité *Il viage entretenido,* d'Agustín de Rojas de Villandrado, comme l'original de notre roman: rien n'est plus inexact. On ne saurait retrouver les traces d'aucune imitation précise. Dans l'œuvre de Rojas, il est, à la vérité, question d'acteurs ambulants, qui vont péniblement gagner quelques maravedis de ville en ville; mais qu'il y a loin des Ríos, des Solano et des Ramírez, vagabonds et voleurs, au noble personnage de Destin! L'auteur espagnol dans cette œuvre bizarre, toute en récits, composée de prose et de vers, a voulu laisser surtout des souvenirs personnels sur sa vie aventureuse de comédien; et Scarron aurait été bien empêché d'y trouver quelque ressource pour la peinture des excellents Manceaux et de la troupe de campagne qui vint s'installer dans leurs murs. Tout au plus, à supposer qu'il ait lu le *Voyage* de Rojas, a-t-il pu emprunter à l'auteur espagnol l'idée de mettre des comédiens dans un roman: voilà tout. Cette première idée a même pu lui venir tout aussi bien à la lecture de Quevedo: ne trouve-t-on pas dans le *Buscón* l'histoire d'une troupe d'acteurs qui courent les grands chemins de l'Espagne? Pablo ne s'engage-t-il pas dans la compagnie, séduit pas les beaux yeux d'une actrice, tout comme Léandre se fait comédien pour suivre sa chère Angélique? Mais encore une fois, ce sont là des rencontres fortuites; et le roman de Scarron, dans les détails comme dans l'ensemble, n'a été tiré d'aucun livre espagnol. [16]

Paul Morillot then proceeds to compare the intrigue without order of the Spanish picaresque novel to that of the *Roman comique*. Lazarillo de Tormes' adventures are compared to those of Ragotin. Turning to *Don Quijote,* Morillot admits that Scarron had read the work and admired the genius of Cervantes. However, he

---

[15] J. Demogeot, *Histoire des literatures estrangeres. Literatures meridionales: Italie-Espagne* (Paris: Librairie Hachette, 1892), pp. 380-381.
[16] Paul Morillot, *Scarron et le genre burlesque* (Paris: H. Lecève et H. Oudin, éditeurs, 1888), p. 343.

denies there is any actual influence, if not the title of some chapters. Morillot concludes his analysis of Spanish sources stating:

> Voilà tout ce que Scarron a pris à l'Espagne: peut-être lui doit-il la première idée de son livre, sous la forme la plus vague, quoique cela ne soit nullement prouvé; il lui doit probablement le désordre impertinent de l'intrigue; il lui doit à coup sûr les nouvelles qu'il a intercalées comme des hors-d'œuvre dans le récit. Mais, quant à cette peinture des caractères, qui fait le mérite original de l'œuvre, Scarron n'en est redevable qu'à son propre génie, et aussi à de lointains souvenirs. [17]

However, in the appendix to his work, *Scarron et le genre burlesque*, Morillot includes an interesting note written anonymously. Here is part of it:

> Je luy dis qu'il falloit donc qu'il entreprist quelque ouvrage de son chef et de son caractère enjoué plustot que cette morale de Gassendy trop serieuse pour lui, et qu'il y meslast des nouvelles dont je luy fournirois les originaux en espagnol qu'il entendoit et dont j'avois quantité, en quoy il imiteroit au moins don Quixote qui en donne quatres si jolies dans sa premiere partie, de sorte que je puis dire que le public m'a en quelque sorte l'obligation de cet agreable ouvrage, bien que je n'en sois pas l'auteur, aussy bien que de ses quatre dernieres nouvelles imprimées à part. [18]

In addition to comparing the four *nouvelles* to those in *Don Quijote*, Scarron's friend had previously suggested that he translate Cervantes' novel, an idea that was rejected since Scarron wanted to write something original. Thus, it is very possible that in writing his novel, Scarron had *Don Quijote* in mind. In fact, there is a great resemblance in theme as pointed out by Adolphe de Puibusque:

> Le *Roman comique*, en effet, quelque graveleux qu'il fut, renfermait une satire très-divertissante et très-opportune; il remporta la même victoire sur les romans de métaphy-

---

[17] *Ibid.*, p. 344.
[18] *Ibid.*, p. 405.

sique amoureuse, que l'œuvre de Cervantès, sur les romans de rêverie chevaleresque.[19]

The *Roman comique* resembles Cervantes' work not only in the fact that it has similar chapter headings, but also in that it has a similar purpose or theme, and that both contain four interpolated stories. This resemblance will have great significance in the discussion of the four interpolated stories, which is the purpose of this work.

The Spanish texts will be compared to the French version by Scarron in order to determine the changes that were made. These changes will help us understand the purpose Scarron had in mind when placing them in the text, which in turn will lead to the question of how they fit in the total structure of the *Roman comique,* while keeping in mind that it was fashioned after the famous work of Cervantes.

Before proceeding in this analysis, two works should be mentioned, since one deals with the relationship of the French stories to the whole novel, while the other discusses some of the changes that Scarron made in his translation.

Most critics who have dealt with the four interpolated stories in the *Roman comique* have stated that they have no relation to the rest of the novel and are only included to provide variety or to provide some satisfaction to those who only care for romantic adventures. Emile Magne, for example, in *Scarron et son milieu,* while discussing the anonymous note in which the author takes credit for the four interpolated stories, states, naming the anonymous author:

> Cabart de Villermont: *Note d'un annoyme précipitée,* se vante d'avoir incliné Scarron à placer, dans le *Roman comique,* les nouvelles tirées de l'espagnol qui y figurent. Son influence fut, sur ce point, déplorable.[20]

Hainsworth is the first to point out that these stories are not completely extraneous, since they are as romanesque as the tale

---

[19] Adolphe de Puibusque, *Histoire comparée des literatures espagnole et française* (Paris: Chez G. A. Dentu, 1843), II, 173.

[20] Emile Magne, *Scarron et son milieu* (Paris: Emile Paul frères, éditeurs, 1924), p. 162.

of Destin and Estoile, and that Scarron also adds the same comical devices to them so that they are in tone similar to the rest of the novel. [21]

Ernest Simon, in "The Function of the Spanish Stories in Scarron's *Roman comique*," tries to link the four stories to the general structure. However, he only discusses the first one, the "Histoire de l'amante invisible" and concludes that these tales are a parody of the heroic and sentimental novels of the time. He ties this satire with Scarron's satire on Ragotin and then states:

> The purpose of all this banter, and of the link between Ragotin and the Spanish stories, is the confrontation of two extremes. Because they are nothing but fiction, contrivance, pure invention, the tales are privileged to portray a world whose inhabitants have no other business but love, and where they can pursue this exclusive business without interruption from the usual contingencies of life, which are eliminated by the author-creator's providential intervention. This situation is the exact reversal of Ragotin's predicament, where the love quest is continually frustrated by an endless series of petty contingencies. Scarron succeeded in including in his novel both the romantic extreme of a conventional literary treatment of love, and the equally extreme burlesque of that literary convention. [22]

Ernest Simon's parallel is an interesting one. However, he has not taken into account the other three *novelas,* and he has not compared this one with the Spanish original in order to see more clearly Scarron's changes and try to explain them as an effort to fit these stories into the *Roman comique.*

One more work should be mentioned before attempting an analysis of the four *novelas*: R. Cadorel's *Scarron et la nouvelle espagnole dans le "Roman comique."* This work is useful in that it presents side by side the Spanish and the French versions, and thus it is easy to perceive the changes even if the Spanish version has been translated into French. In addition, a short analysis is made of Scarron's changes. These changes are viewed *per se* and not in relation to the rest of the novel, since Cadorel states:

---

[21] Hainsworth, *op. cit.*, pp. 170-193.
[22] Ernest Simon, "The Function of the Spanish Stories in Scarron's *Roman comique*," *L'Esprit Créateur,* III (Fall, 1963), pp. 130-136.

L'action des Nouvelles reste entièrement différente de celle du *Roman Comique,* et il serait vain de chercher, entre celles-ci et le Roman, une unité qui n'existe à aucun moment. [23]

Also, Cadorel first analyzes "A trompeur, trompeur et demi," as if the source were "A un engaño, otro mayor." This, of course, is inaccurate. At the end of the chapter he adds the following note which as will be seen later is also mistaken:

Au moment même où le tirage de ce mémoire commence, une lecture opportune vient de nous révéler que, contrairement à ce qu'on pense..., cette nouvelle n'a pas pour modèle "A un engaño otro mayor," qui se trouve dans le recueil "Los Alivios de Casandra," mais bien la troisième et dernière des nouvelles insérées dans "La Garduña de Sevilla" dont le titre est "A lo que obliga el Honor." Il ne peut y avoir aucun doute possible à ce sujet; il s'agit, en tous points, d'une traduction littérale qui suit exactement le texte espagnol. [24]

Some of the conclusions made by Cadorel are valid even when Scarron's *nouvelles* are considered in relation to the rest of the *Roman comique.* These conclusions are stated also in this work but are expanded. First, Cadorel mentions Scarron's move toward Classicism. Second, also as does G. Hainsworth, Cadorel points to the humorous additions made by Scarron. And finally, but more importantly, Cadorel notices how Victoria, in the second interpolated story, emerges as a stronger character than she was in Castillo Solórzano, although he gives no explanation for this.

These are then the most significant works on the subject. Let us now turn to the text and analyze Scarron's changes, and explain them as an effort to fit the Spanish *novelas* into the *Roman comique* by having them fit into the action of the novel.

---

[23] R. Cadorel, *Scarron et la nouvelle espagnole dans le "Roman comique"* (Aix-en-Provence: La Pensée Universitaire, 1960), p. 6.
[24] *Ibid.*

Chapter II

L'AMANTE INVISIBLE

Los alivios de Casandra, a collection of short stories, appeared in Madrid in the year 1640. The author, Alonso Castillo Solórzano, was an extremely popular writer in Spain at the time, having by then written more than twenty titles. He specialized in these short stories, so the appearance of this collection was no surprise. What is particularly significant about it, is the popularity it gained abroad. His other works had not had such a reception.

Throughout the seventeenth century this collection remained very popular. Authors such as Vanel, Hauteroche, Nanteuil, Boisrobert, d'Ouville, Roger L'Estrange, and Thomas Otway, translated or imitated one or more of the stories in this collection. One story in particular, "Los efectos que hace amor," became extremely popular. It was used by Paul Scarron in his *Roman comique* as the first of four interpolated stories. Two other stories in this novel are based on stories by Castillo Solórzano, while the fourth is by María de Zayas y Sotomayor, a contemporary and friend of Castillo Solórzano.

This chapter will investigate how Scarron changed the Spanish story, "Los efectos que hace amor," the reason for the changes, and the reason for including the story in the *Roman comique.*

In contrast to the realistic and satiric tone of the *Roman comique,* "Los efectos que hace amor" is a serious, idealized, and romanesque story. The author revels in mysterious circumstances, dark nigths, narrow streets, masked ladies, magnificent palaces, and ideal love. The plot is well constructed since it maintains the reader's interest, and dazzles him at every turn, surprising him in the end with an extraordinary but very well thought-out conclusion. The story is more romantic or fantastic than many of Castillo Solórzano's *novelas*. In fact, it is stated in *Los alivios de Casandra* that Diana, the narrator, was congratulated for having constructed a short story that pleased more than the others for being "ingeniosa y extraordinaria." [1]

The story takes place in Naples, where a magnificent celebration is being given. Many nobles from other countries are present. One in particular, Carlos de Aragón, has distinguished himself for his bravery in the games and tourneys, and also for being extremely handsome and rich, coming from a very noble family.

One day in church he meets a masked lady who tells him how much she admires him, and that she would like to know him better. When Carlos agrees, and admires her ability to converse wittily, she disappears. Eight days later, Carlos is walking home at night and is called aside by a woman. She is inside a house and talks to him from behind a *reja*. She is of course the mysterious lady he had seen previously. Carlos asks her to reveal her identity, but she will neither tell him her name nor remove her mask. They meet in the same place every night, and Carlos falls madly in love with her.

At a ball, he thinks he recognizes his "invisible" lady and goes to talk to her. He soon realizes his mistake, but the invisible lady, who was also there, becomes jealous, although she does not later admit to him that she was at the ball. She decides that she must act soon or lose Carlos.

The scene changes to the church, where Carlos meets another masked lady, who tells him that she is in love with him and will not tolerate his nocturnal expeditions. That night, while Carlos is speaking to the invisible lady, four men surprise and kidnap him. He is taken to a beautiful palace, where he meets the most beautiful lady he has ever seen. She tells him she is the Princess Porcia, the lady he had met that same day at the church, and she will keep him there until he decides to marry her.

Although Carlos is taken by her beauty, riches, and charm, he tells the Princess he is going to be faithful to his invisible lady. A letter from her arrives, thanks to a bribed servant. Carlos acquires

---

[1] Alonso de Castillo Solórzano, *Los alivios de Casandra* (Barcelona: Emprenta de Jayme Romeo, 1640), pp. 85-86.

new courage, and finally persuades the Princess to let him go and that she is only wasting her time.

That night he goes to see his invisible lady who is waiting for him. She agrees to remove her mask, but to do this they must go to another place. The invisible lady conducts Carlos to a beautiful palace and removes her mask. It turns out that she is Princess Porcia, and that she had been only testing his faithfulness. That night they are married.

In addition to such a florid and romantic plot, the style and descriptions are very elaborate and lengthy. Thus, the question is how Scarron was able to fit such a story into a realistic and satiric work, written in a very direct and clear style, and not at all concerned with romantic adventures, but dealing instead with a wandering troupe of actors in the French countryside.

John Dryden classifies translations as being done either through metaphrase or word for word translation, paraphrase, or imitation. Paraphrase is defined by Dryden as: "Where the author is kept in view by the translator, so as never to be lost, but his words are not so strictly followed as his sense; and that too is admitted to be amplified, but not altered."[2] Any further changes constitute imitation. If this classification is accepted, Scarron then imitated Castillo Solórzano. However, the Spanish originals do not undergo radical alterations. This work will discuss first the mechanical changes, and then the changes in ideas.

Although "L'Amante invisible" is an imitation and not a paraphrase of Castillo Solórzano, there is a surprising accuracy of detail, which raises the possibility that although Scarron did not stick to the text of the original, he must have had the original in front of him for reference, and not trusted to his memory. Scarron tries to give the impression that he is recounting a story that he heard or read a long time before. For example, Castillo Solórzano states the story takes place during the reign of Philip IV, while Scarron states: "...aux nopces de Philippes second, troisiesme ou quatriesme, car je ne sçay pas lequel."[2] This is also pointed out by Hainsworth.[4]

---

[2] William Frost, *Dryden and the Art of Translation* (New Haven: Yale University Press, 1955), p. 31.

[3] Paul Scarron, *Le Roman comique* in *Romanciers du XVIIe siècle*, Antoine Adam éd. (Paris: Bibliothèque de la Pléiade, 1962), p. 552.

"L'AMANTE INVISIBLE" 31

This off-hand attitude will be discussed later. All that must be noted now is that Scarron must have had the text in front of him, even though he tries to give a different impression. Ragotin, in the following chapter of the *Roman comique,* is very proud of having recounted the story so successfully, but someone takes from his pocket a small book that happens to be the original story written by someone else:

> Un jeune homme, dont j'ay oublié le nom, luy répondit qu'elle n'estoit pas à luy plustost qu'à un autre puisqu'il l'avoit prise dans un livre; et en disant cela, il en fit voir un qui sortoit à demy hors de la pochette de Ragotin et s'en saisit brusquement. [5]

Ragotin represents Scarron in this episode. Scarron, in his satire, will not neglect himself as an object of satire; and just as Ragotin, he knows that he is taking credit for someone else's work. A few years later, this episode in the *Roman comique* will become true since someone will bring out the original Spanish story and accuse Scarron of having taken credit for something that is not his. This person will be d'Ouville. Scarron's foresight will also be seen in the discussion of the drama that follows the fight over Ragotin's book. This will be discussed later.

Many examples of this accuracy in detail are found in the story. In Castillo Solórzano, eight days elapse between the time the invisible lady meets Carlos at the church, and the time she signals to Carlos when he is on his way home after he has been gambling. [6] The same is true in Scarron: eight days go by, and he has been gambling. [7]

Two ladies are present when Carlos visits the church for a second time, and meets what appears to be a diferent lady in "Los efectos que hace amor." The same number of ladies are present in Scarron. Another instance where the numbers are the same occurs when Carlos is kidnapped. In both versions he is kidnapped by four

---

[4] G. Hainsworth, *Les "Novelas Ejemplares" de Cervantes en France au XVIIe siècle* (Paris: Librairie Ancienne Honoré Champion, 1933), p. 181.

[5] Scarron, *op. cit.,* p. 567.

[6] Castillo Solórzano, *op. cit.,* p. 65.

[7] Scarron, *op. cit.,* p. 554.

men while he is talking to the invisible lady. Also, in both versions it takes the kidnapper an hour to travel to Princess Porcia's place.[8]

There are many other instances of surprising coincidence of detail. Courtship is compared to a combat or duel by the invisible lady. She gives as a reason for her absence of eight days the fact she had to find out whether he was free, since only that way they could "duel" on equal terms. Compare both passages:

> El requisito de los desafíos es pelear siempre con armas iguales; y a quien lo haze con ventaja, se le acusa de covarde. Yo he querido entrar en campo con vos igualmente, se que las armas que puedo llevar son de sencilla libertad y que no tengo el cuydado puesto en parte alguna: salir vos a batalla conmigo con otro empleo, era no solo salir yo vencida pero agraviada; he procurado saber si en vuestra armeria teneys armas deste genero, que me puedan ofender.[9]

> Vous scavez que dans les combat assignez il se faut battre avec armes pareilles; si vostre cœur n'estoit pas aussy libre que le mien, vous vous batteriez avec avantage; et c'est pour cela que j'ay voulu m'informer de vous.[10]

Carlos then argues that if they are going to fight with similar weapons, she should let him know who she is, since not letting him know gives her an unfair advantage. She avoids the central argument in the question, and contends she must maintain secrecy in order that he may merit her. But, she adds to soothe him, that she is not ugly, and that she is as noble as he is. All this is present in both versions:

> Dos cosas me pedís, dijo ella, en que no os podré por ahora daros gusto, tened paciencia, que quiero que merezcays con ella, sirviéndome sin pretender de mi mas de aquello que os quisiere permitir; y porque se comience este galanteo con fundamento, desde luego os aseguro que os igualo en calidad, que tengo suficiente hazienda para vivir en Napoles con la ostentacion que tiene el mas poderoso Principe de los que aqui assisten, y que mi edad

---

[8] Castillo Solórzano, *op. cit.*, p. 71; Scarron, *op. cit.*, p. 559.
[9] Castillo Solórzano, *op. cit.*, p. 66.
[10] Scarron, *op. cit.*, p. 554.

es poca, pues del rostro no os digo que el es, basta certificaros que es un medio la hermosura, y que se arrima mas a la superior que a la común.[11]

Esperez sans impatience, c'est par là que vous pouvez meriter ce que vous pretendez de moy, qui vous assure (afin que vostre galanterie ne soit pas sans fondement et sans espoir de recompense) que je vous esgale en condition, que j'ai assez de bien pour vous faire vivre avecque autant d'eclat que le plus grand Prince du Royaume, que je suis jeune, que je suis plus belle que laide.[12]

A final example: Scarron keeps in his narrative an insignificant part that is however very indicative of the Spanish nature of the story. This is the "engaño con la verdad". Carlos is at Porcia's house, and she states that she nows his secret lady, and that if a comparison were made, she would not be at all inferior to the invisible lady. This is true since Porcia and the invisible lady are the same person, but such a statement serves to deceive the reader and Carlos:

Mi verguenza me ha costado este arrojamiento y quiero que de mi sepays que ni en calidad, belleza, ni estado me excede: con esto os quedad con Dios que estoy cierta que no me abreys desatisfazer, sino confesar que esto es verdad.[13]

Et puisque je me suis declarée, qui vais si bien luy rompre tous ses desseins que j'emporteray sur elle une victoire que j'ay droit de luy disputer, puisque je ne luy suis point inférieure ny en beute, ny en richesses, ny en qualité ny en tout ce qui rend une personne aimable.[14]

Yet, even though there are these surprisingly accurate details preserved in the French version, Scarron's version is an imitation and not a paraphrase. Consequently, there are many differences in detail. As stated before, Scarron declares the public celebration in Naples took place during the reign of one of the Philips, but he

---

[11] Solórzano, *op. cit.*, p. 66.
[12] Scarron, *op. cit.*, p. 555.
[13] Castillo Solórzano, *op. cit.*, p. 71.
[14] Scarron, *op. cit.*, p. 558.

does not know which one. This detail has already been referred to, and it has been stated that Castillo Solórzano specifically stated Philip IV. This accurate (Scarron remembers it was a Philip) inaccuracy adds to the easy informal style of Scarron, which contrasts with the serious and ornate style of Castillo Solórzano. Also, it might be seen as a criticism of the historical background of the novels of the time; but this will be discussed later. More important now is the fact that Scarron goes on to say that the festival is taking place to celebrate the wedding of the king. Castillo Solórzano states the festival commemorates the "jura de nuevo rey," [15] that is, when Philip IV became King. The reason for the change might be that this way history and story are both conceived with the idea of marriage as the center. This again reflects on the heroic novel of the time in which love and marriage were the cause of every action, on the part of Kings and princesses. Affairs of state were subordinated to love affairs.

As stated before, Scarron was usually accurate with numbers. However, this was not always true. The invisible lady came with two other ladies to the church in Scarron's version, while there were four in Castillo Solórzano's story.

There are also two more significant differences in detail. In Castillo Solórzano, between the first and second meeting of Carlos with the invisible lady, he tries to find out who she is, by finding out who owns the house from where she speaks. It turns out that the house is owned by a very old widow and that no one else lives there. The same search and the same outcome are found in Scarron. However, in the French version Carlos waits until after the second meeting to try to find out who the invisible lady is. The intense interest of Carlos and his delay in trying to discover who the invisible lady was, seems incongruous. Scarron recounts this incident almost as an afterthought; this represents a possible flaw in plot construction and in motivation.

Another difference found in Scarron that also weakens the plot construction and the motivation of "L'Amante invisible" is the fact that the ball took place only two nights after they had met, while

---

[15] Castillo Solórzano, *op. cit.,* p. 62.

Castillo Solórzano allows for more time, thus extending the love affair so that his faithfulness and their future marriage may not appera as an impromptu happening.

Another variation occurs when Carlos meets a beautiful lady at the ball. In Castillo Solórzano there is hesitation on the part of Carlos. He is human in that he is drawn to the lady at the ball, although he finally rejects her. There is no hesitation in Scarron. This may reflect the attitude of a Cornelian hero, or of a hero of the heroic French novel, but it certainly does not add anything to this particular plot, since in Solórzano it is the realization on the part of the invisible lady that Carlos is human (she was also present at the ball) that triggers the second half of the story. This human quality of Carlos in Solórzano's version can be seen in part of his conversation with the lady at the ball:

> Ella le preguntó que como se atrevia a hablarla allí, teniendo dama a quien dar celos, y el respondió a esto, que estava seguro de darlos, porque no tenia dama que se ofendiese.[16]

There are times, however, when these variations do not arise out of carelessness in plot construction, but are improvements on the original. When Carlos is at Porcia's palace and she asks him to gives up the unknown or invisible lady for her, Carlos answere in Castillo Solorzano's version:

> Una costumbre continuada no me negareys que ha menester tiempo para que mude de hábito, confieso que a los principios del primero empleo, me era de algun desabrimiento que me significase su amor quien queria pagas del con fe de que avia de ser hermosa en mi conceto, continue el hablarla, y sus agasajos, y favores echaron tales raices en mi voluntad, que aora dudo, aun con lo que veo de variar el gusto, la causa es aver puesto la voluntad muy deveras en este sugeto aunque no conocido.[17]

Scarron's answer is at the same time more clever and more to the point, while also clearer and shorter, improving the Spanish version:

---

[16] Castillo Solórzano, *op. cit.*, p. 68.
[17] *Ibid.*, p. 79.

> Mais, Madame, m'auriez-vous trouvé digne de votre affection si vous m'aviez crû capable d'estre infidele? Et pourrois-je estre fidele si je vous pouvois aymer? Plaignez-moy, Madame, sans me blamer ou plus tost, plaignons-nous ensemble, vous de ne pouvoir obtenir ce que vous desirez et moy de ne voir point ce que j'ayme. [18]

Some of these differences in detail are simply omissions, where Scarron believes that a particular point will not appeal to a French audience. The belief in magic, so prevalent in Spain, does not seem to have attracted Scarron. In Castillo Solórzano, the invisible lady sends a letter to Carlos while he is a "prisoner" of Porcia in which she states that she has found out his whereabouts through the use of magic:

> Hame costado mucho desuelo y cuydado saber donde estés, porque despues de hazer las diligencias posibles para esto, por mis criados, me he valido de la mágica, a quien nada se encubre, quien la profesa con eminencia, y la usa con muchos que la siguen en este reyno (como tu bien sabras) me dio noticia que en esa quinta te tenia la Princesa Porcia. [19]

Her statement is not present in Scarron. The only allusion to magic in the invisible lady's letter to Carlos is the use of the word "enchantements" when she refers to Porcia. Of course, this does not necessarily reflect the use of magic.

Another important difference between the Spanish version and the French "translation" is the simplification of description in Scarron. Castillo Solórzano begins "Los efectos que hace amor" with a description of the city of Naples which takes up almost a page. No such description is found in Scarron. Leaving out this description, he begins with the facts of the story: Don Carlos is in Naples, and the city is having a celebration. This simplification and directness lead to clarity, an essential quality of French Classicism. It is also in direct contrast with the descriptions found in the French novels of the time.

---

[18] Scarron, *op. cit.*, p. 562.
[19] Castillo Solórzano, *op. cit.*, p. 81.

Castillo Solórzano's tale proceeds with a description of don Carlos, following the description of the city:

> Era don Carlos de edad de veynte y quatro años, de lindo talle, hermoso rostro, proporcionados miembros, muy discreto musico, Poeta, y grande hombre de acaballo en las dos sillas. [20]

Again, we do not find a description in Scarron. For him, Carlos is just the hero of a typical heroic novel of the time. Such a hero did not need to be described, since the imagination of the reader could certainly produce even better results.

The art of conversation was just as important in Spain as it was in France at this time. Endless conversations appeared in the French heroic romances of the seventeenth century. Endless conversations took place in the salons. However, Scarron, although witty, had no room in his realistic work for the florid expressions of great lovers and heroes. The long conversations found in "Los efectos que hace amor" are here simplified, particularly the long love dialogues or love duels. A good example of this is the first conversation between Carlos and the invisible lady at the church. [21]

Many metaphors and similes are also reduced or eliminated in Scarron. Some that are particularly significant though, like the idea of courting as a duel, remain. But extraneous or superfluous comparisons that serve only to enhance the language are eliminated. The following expression found in Castillo Solórzano is totally absent in Scarron: "Pues en los colores que sacastes se vió quan libre estays de las flechas de Cupido." [22]

Another such comparison found in the story of Castillo Solórzano and absent in *Le Roman comique* is the following:

> Ella dijo...os doy my gaje en esa sortija, quitose un guante, y descubrió un pedazo de cristal animado, que eso parecía una de sus hermosas manos, y de uno de sus blancos dedos saco una sortija de diamantes. [23]

---

[20] *Ibid.*, p. 62.
[21] Castillo Solórzano, *op. cit.*, p. 63; Scarron, *op. cit.*, p. 553.
[22] Castillo Solórzano, *op. cit.*, p. 63.
[23] *Ibid.*, p. 65.

The best example of this simplification of description can be seen when Porcia takes of her mask, and the author tries to describe what Carlos sees. The difference in both length and type of description is apparent here:

> Quitó a este tiempo la dama un botón a la mascarilla que llevava, y descubrio un cielo abreviado, asi lo juzgó don Carlos, en el hermoso espacio de una proporcionada, y blanca frente, descubrio dos yris de brunido azabache, arcos con que amor asegurara mas rendimientos que con el instrumento corbo con que rinde las almas, eran estas adorno de dos hermosos ojos negros, y rasgados, de quien el mayor planeta podia pedir prestadas luzes, las mejillas vertian púrpura y nieve, con una divina mezcla, tal que la naturaleza se admiró cuando formo tal obra de sus manos; dividia sus hermosos capos una proporcionada línea, realce hermoso de sus bellos primores, en cuya vezindad campeava las perfecciones de un clavel dividido, tal era su hermosisima boca, de su librea se vistieron las bellas guardas de dos hilos de perlas mas perfectas que las que engendra el Sur, la barba no desdecía de lo pintado, antes era hermoso aumento de sus divinas perfecciones, era atlante deste breve cielo una hermosa y gentil columna de cristal, tal era su divina garganta.... [24]

> Elle se demasqua et fit voir a Dom Carlos les cieux ouverts ou, si vouls voulez, le ciel en petit, la plus belle teste du monde, soustenue par un corps de la plus riche taille qu'il eust jamais admirée. [25]

Notice that Scarron pretends to want to say "les cieux ouverts", a common expression, but he then adds "le ciel en petit" as a concession to the reader. This expression is taken from Castillo Solórzano, so that in making this concession Scarron is criticizing the type of description found in the Spanish version and in the French fiction of the time.

Another diference between the writings of Castillo Solórzano and Scarron is in the direct approach to the subject of the latter. This should already be apparent from the previous discussion, and the previous examples should also serve to illustrate this characteristic.

---

[24] *Ibid.*, p. 78.
[25] Scarron, *op. cit.*, p. 562.

The fact that Castillo Solórzano begins with a description of Naples while the author of the *Roman comique* begins with facts that are necessary to the plot is certainly an example of this. Also, the lack of hesitation shown by Carlos in Scarron's version when he sees the lady at the ball, shows this direct approach.

Scarron does not want to deal with side issues, but wants to present a straightforward plot in a concise manner, going from beginning to end in a precise and direct way.

A final example of this characteristic occurs when Carlos and the invisible lady are discussing the love duel. She states in both versions that they both have to have equal arms. However, in Castillo Solórzano, the invisible lady adds that if this is not so, she will not only be defeated but also "agraviada".[25] This concept of honor is essential to the Spanish viewpoint. However, in adapting the story, Scarron realized this was an concept that did not add to the resolution of the plot. Any extraneous concept must be eliminated.

A more important diference between both versions, because it adds a personal flavor to the story written by Scarron, is the extra humor found in the French version. There is no hint of humor in Castillo Solórzano. He is recounting an idealized and romantic story about love. No humor can be admitted. Scarron uses a different approach. For all his lack of seriousness and for all his humor, he is more didactic than Castillo Solórzano, since he has something to tell us and he is not just writing a romantic tale for entertainment. Even Scarron's humor is there to make the reader think. It also makes an ornate and heavy story light and witty.

One phase of this humor is coupled with Scarron's moralizing vein. Castillo Solórzano simply mentions that Carlos and the invisible lady met at a church:

> Entró un dia don Carlos en Santiago de los Españoles, que esta en su quartel, y despues de aver oido alli Misa, al querer salirse fue llamando de quatro bizarras damas.[27]

Scarron on the other hand condemns and ridicules young men and women who attend church only to meet each other:

---

[26] Castillo Solórzano, *op. cit.*, p. 66.
[27] *Ibid.*, p. 63.

> On prophane les Eglises en ce pays-là aussy bien qu'au nôtre, ... on y devroit donner ordre etablir des chasse-gadelureaux et des chasse-coquettes dans les eglises, comme des chasse-chiens et des chasse-chiennes. [28]

This can be considered as one of the many satiric references on the novel found in this story, since in sentimental novels of this time men and women noticed each other and met in church. However, it is included in this thesis under the general category of humor, since it was not just a novelistic technique, and Scarron may have been attacking this widespread custom as Antoine Adam states:

> Scarron ne se moque pas ici des romans contemporains où les rencontres dans les églises sont de tradition. Il relève un usage alors général. Les gens du bel air avaient dans les églises une tenue très libre. Ils y allaient, comme dit une *Critique agréable de Paris* "pour se divertir, pour parler et se faire l'amour." [29]

Another example of humor in Scarron's version of "Los efectos que hace amor" occurs in the first conversation between the invisible lady and Carlos in the church. Hainsworth points out this paragraph and states: "Parfois, se donnant des airs d'historien véridique, Scarron affecte de n'être pas exactement renseigné sur tel détail concernant ses personnages." [30] After a short repartee, Scarron adds:

> Ils se dirent encore cent belles choses, que je ne vous diray point, parce que je ne les sçay pas et que je n'ay garde de vous en composer d'autres, de peur de faire tort à Dom Carlos et à la Dame Inconnue, qui avoient bien plus d'esprit que je n'en ay. [31]

This again may be a satirical comment on the writers of novels of the time since these works were saturated with elegant conversations, witty repartee, and long discourses on or about love. However, it may also be a comment, like the above mentioned satire

---

[28] Scarron, *op. cit.*, p. 552.
[29] Scarron, *op. cit.*, p. 1423.
[30] Hainsworth, *op. cit.*, p. 181.
[31] Scarron, *op. cit.*, p. 553.

on the church, on contemporary customs. It is well known that the seventeenth century is a century when conversation was of great importance. The salons rewarded those that could converse brilliantly by admitting them and making them well known. To succeed in the literary salon, more than the knowledge of literature and the ability to write was needed. One had to call attention to oneself through conversation. This importance of conversation was exported to England at the time of the Restoration of Charles II, creating the restoration comedy, where conversations between the man and the woman became duels of words in which the woman had to defead her adversary in order to marry him. The mention of the love duel in this story by Scarron may have been what attracted Thomas Otway's attention and led him to write *The Atheist,* a typical restoration comedy based on the story of the invisible lady. However, there, as in most restoration comedies, plot became relegated to the love duel.

In the Spanish story, this conversation or love duel is more important than in the French version, although it does not attain the importance that it will in England. Thus, Scarron is satirizing in this passage several things: the Spanish *novela,* the French novel, and French customs. If indeed he is directing his attention to the French novel in this comment, the statement that the heroes have more "esprit" or kit than he has, is certainly a direct attack on the authors of novels who apparently do not have as much with as the poeple who attend the salons.

Another example in which the author of the *Roman comique* introduces humor to satirize a custom of the times is when he tries to find out who the girl at the ball was, and is told that she is:

> ...la fille d'un Marquis de je ne sçay quel Marquisat; car c'est la chose du monde dont je voudrois le moins jurer, en un temps où tout le monde se Marquise de soy mesme, je veux dire de son chef. [32]

Here Scarron is criticizing the prevalent custom of usurping titles. This custom will exist throughout the century; in 1675, Mme

---

[32] *Ibid.,* p. 556.

de Sévigné will write: "Quand un homme veut usurper un titre, ce n'est point celui de comte, c'est celui de marquis." [33]

Other than the customs, Scarron uses his humor in the description of the hero Carlos. During the first meeting with Carlos, the invisible lady reveals she equals him in nobility, and she is not ugly. With these words, she departs suddenly, leaving Carlos in amazement. The word for amazement in the Spanish version is "admirado". [34] The French version states that the invisible lady left, "laissant Dom Carlos la bouche ouverte." [35] It is rather incongruous for the hero of a sentimental work to be left with his mouth open. Here Scarron is satirizing his own hero, is ridiculing the pompous seriousness of the heroes of novels, and perhaps even the seriousness of the young man of his time who tried to act as if he was a hero of a sentimental novel.

Another instance in which Scarron ridicules his hero occurs when he is taken prisoner by Princess Porcia. As the carriage arrives at her palace, the four masked men conduct Carlos inside:

> Les quatre mascarades descendirent du carrosse avecque Dom Carlos, le tenant par-dessous les bras, comme un Ambassadeur introduit à saluer le Grand Seigneur. [36]

The heroic and sentimental man of the novels of the seventeenth century must have certainly felt the ridiculous position in which Carlos found himself. Again, this is a satire on the novel and possibly on those people that dreamed they were like such heroes. Again, it is also a satire on the seriousness with which Castillo de Solórzano presents Carlos, and the seriousness with which he describes Porcia's palace.

Humor is also used at the end of the short story to destroy the efect that has been built up slowly. In spite of all the satirical statements, Carlos and Porcia emerge at the end of the story as two perfect lovers who deserve each other. Castillo Solórzano ends the story with happiness and marriage. The marriage of course demands a sumptuous and majestic feast. In Scarron there is an added line;

---

[33] *Ibid.*, p. 1424.
[34] Castillo Solórzano, *op. cit.*, p. 66.
[35] Scarron, *op. cit.*, p. 555.
[36] Scarron, *op. cit.*, p. 559.

after the wedding, "on dit qu'ils se levèrent bien tard le lendemain; ce que je n'ay pas grand peine à croire." [37] This points to the fact that the purpose of all the artifices, witty dialogues, and enchanted palaces was to enable them to go to bed with each other; and the next morning they did not rise until late, which is to be expected of any *human* beings in their position.

A more important function of the French version, and one that it shares with the rest of the *Roman comique* is satire against novels of the time. The *novela* by Castillo Solórzano can be seen as a miniature of the French novel of the seventeenth century: a prince who after many fantastic adventures is reunited with his beloved and marries her. The story is also an imitation in miniature of the romances of chivalry in the idea that a man must merit his lady: he must show his valor and virtue before she will consent to have anything to do with him. These novels of chivalry stand as the basis for the sentimental and heroic French novels of the seventeenth century.

The witty conversation, as pointer out before, is another main aspect of the novels. It is present in the short story.

Scarron chose a perfect miniature example of what a typical novel is like, except that the story has unity of action and is not episodic, saturated with extraneous récits. Scarron, in ridiculing the short story, is also ridiculing the novel.

The fact that Scarron is trying to satirize both novels in general and the story of Castillo Solórzano in particular, is obvious if we read the beginning of the first chapter of the *Roman comique* and compare it to one of many similar description in "Los alivios de Casandra":

> A penas el luciente planeta comenzo a declinar en su curso menguando luzes, y dilatando sombras, encaminando su flamigero carro al oceano donde esperaba sepultar esplandores en monumentos de Zafir, quando la hermosisima Casandra.... [38]
>
> Le soleil avoit achevé plus de la moitié de sa course et son char, ayant attrappé le penchant du monde, roulloit

---

[37] *Ibid.*, p. 559.
[38] Castillo Solórzano, *op. cit.*, p. 6.

> plus viste qu'il vouloit. Si ses chevaux eussent voulu profiter de la pente du chemin, ils eussent achevé ce qui restoit du jour en moins d'un demy-quart d'heure: Mais au lieu de tirer de toute leur force, ils ne s'amusoient qu'a faire des courbettes, respirant un air marin qui les fasoit hannir et les advertisoit que la mer estoit proche, ou l'on dit que leur Maistre se couche toutes les nuits. Pour parler plus humainement et plus intelligible, il estoit entre cinq et six quand une charette entra dans les Halles du Mans. [39]

Since satire on the novel is one fo the most important purpose of the interpolated story in Scarron, several examples should be given of this. An example already mentioned several times is that at the beginning of the *nouvelle* Scarron mentions that it takes place during the reign of one of the Philips, although he does not remember which one. This is an attack on the heroic novel of the time where the author chose a historical setting as a *cadre,* by naming the hero as the son of a famous king, preferably from the Orient. But other than inventing a few customs, the author did not follow up on the history. This is what Scarron tries to point out when he states that it really does not matter what king the story took place under, since this will not add anything to the story. Also, he fact that Scarron changes the Spanish version to have his story begin with a marriage of the king points to the importance of marriage in these novels. All the heroic feats are performed in order to gain the haud of the beloved.

Later on in the *nouvelle,* Scarron adds a paragraph that is not present in the Spanish version. In this paragraph he is more explicit about the novel. After don Carlos is left open mouthed by the invisible lady, Scarron states:

> Je ne vous diray point exactement s'il avoit soupé, et s'il se coucha sans manger, comme font quelques faiseurs de Romans qui reiglent toutes les heures du jour de leurs Heros, les font lever de bon matin, conter leur Histoire jusqu'à l'heure du disner, disner fort legerement et apres disner reprendre leur Histoire ou s'enfoncer dans un bois pour y parler tous seuls, si ce n'est quand ils ont quelque chose à dire aux arbres et aux rochers ; à l'heure du souper,

---

[39] Scarron, *op. cit.,* p. 532.

> se trouver à point nommé dans le lieu de manger, et puis s'en vont faire des chasteaux en Espagne sur quelque terrasse qui garde la mer, tandis qu'un Escuyer revele que son maistre est un tel, fils d'un Roy tel et qu'il n'y a pas un meilleur Prince.... [40]

The expression "chasteaux en Espagne" should be pointed out. These heroes are men that let their imagination run wild, just as the authors of these novels let their imaginations run wild. What more appropriate hero to build castles in Spain than Don Carlos, who has real castles in Spain? Princess Porcia advises Don Carlos: "Ne croyez pas vostre imagination aux dépens de vostre jugement." [41]

This is the main complaint that Scarron has against the novels, as pointed out by the way he ends the story. Scarron objects to these works because they stimulate the imagination to such an extent that man loses sight of reality. Men believe they are the heroes of novels and lose sight of who and where they are. Porcia, ironically, is giving Don Carlos good advice, but he can not take it since he is a hero in a work of fiction. The resolution will be a happy one also, since it is a work of fiction. However, judgment should be exercised in real life since it is not always idealized. But people like Don Carlos — members of the aristocracy — those with real castles in Spain, may allow themselves the luxury of imagining new "castles". The main danger is for those who have none and can only imagine, since they stand to lose the most.

In describing Porcia's palace, Scarron states that Don Carlos could have used his imagination:

> S'il eust esté de l'humeur de Dom Quixote, il eust trouvé là de quoy s'en donner jusqu'aux gardes et il se fust crû pour le moins Esplandian ou Amadis; mais nostre Espagnol ne s'en esmeut. [42]

However, we have here again the fact that Don Carlos looks at reality and foregoes the dream. The passage shows that Scarron knew the *Don Quijote* of Cervantes. In that work, novels had

---

[40] *Ibid.*, p. 555.
[41] *Ibid.*, p. 558.
[42] *Ibid.*, p. 560.

disordered the mind of one that did not have but could only imagine. Life must be regarded as it is. If Don Carlos, a rich nobleman, does not regard himself as Amadis, why should a bourgeois come to believe that he is a hero of a novel? Men must preserve their contact with the world. Imagination is a dangerous luxury.

In describing the room that may have led Carlos to believe that he was Amadis, Scarron alludes again to the novels in a paragraph completely absent from the Spanish original:

> Je ne vous diray point si les flambeaux que tenoient les Demoiselles estoient d'argent; c'est pour le moins: ils estoient plus tost de vermeil doré cizelé, et la salle estoit la plus magnifique du monde, et, si vous voulez, aussi bien meublée que quelques appartemens de nos Romans, comme le vaisseau de Zelmatide dans le Polexandre, le palais d'Hibraim dans l'Illustre Bassa, ou la chambre où le Roy d'Assyrie receut Mandane, dans le Cyrus, qui est sans doute, aussi bien que les autres que j'ay nommez, le livre du monde le mieux meublé. [43]

This is followed by many references to the romances of chivalry, for example, the mention of "Urgande la deconnue." [44] This close association between the heroic novel and the romances of chivalry in Ssacorron point again to the fact that one of his main objections to these works was the fact that they stimulated the imagination to a point where reality was no longer existent. The romances of chivalry, the French novels, and the *novelas* of Castillo Solórzano all try to ignore man's struggle with his environment and concentrate on something non-existent.

The novels of chivalry are only mentioned once in Castillo Solórzano. When Carlos is in Porcia's palace, the author of "Los alivios de Casandra" states that Carlos did not know how such an adventure would end, "que por tal se podía juzgar como las de los libros de Amadis de Gaula a Esplandian." [45] Castillo Solórzano does not attack the novel of chivalry, only compares Carlos' adventures to the adventures in the romances of chivalry. It was not

---

[43] *Ibid.*, p. 559.
[44] *Ibid.*, p. 561.
[45] Castillo Solórzano, *op. cit.*, p. 76.

Scarron's idea to group them together, since the comparison is made by Castillo Solórzano himself. Scarron, however, added the criticism.

There are many references to the French novels in the French version of Scarron which are not present in Castillo Solórzano. For example, in the letter the invisible lady sends to Carlos when he is a prisoner of Porcia, the invisible lady compares Carlos to Renaud, who is a captive of "dangereuse Armide." [46] Later, Carlos compares Porcia to Citherée. [47] Thus, Scarron's version of Castillo Solorzano's "Los efectos que hace amor," is permeated with allusions to the French novel, which Scarron considers dangerous.

A final question: why does Scarron include the "Histoire de la belle invisible" at this point in the novel, and why does he have Ragotin tell the story? The story of the invisible lady is told just as Ragotin is introduced into the *Roman comique,* in chapter eight; thus, through it, one may expect to get a further insight into his personality. The time spent on the introduction of this character is reasonable since, as Felix Guirard and Andre V. Pierre state in the *Notice* to the Classique Larousse edition of the *Roman comique,* "C'est lui qui occupe le plus grande place dans le *Roman comique,* qui pourrait aussi bien s'intituler *Les malheurs de Ragotin.*" [48]

Scarron describes Ragotin as "un petit homme veuf, Advocat de profession." [49] However, he, just as many bourgeois of the time, had literary ambitions. These ambitions will be later ridiculed and condemned by Furetière in his *Roman bourgeois.* Ragotin, entering into the midst of a company of players with a Spanish *novela* that he wants to turn into "une pièce dans les règles," [50] reminds the reader of Javotte, as she enters a salon and describes the type of sonnet she prefers.

Here the comparison stops. Although Ragotin will fail in everything he tries to accomplish, he does not fail with the "Histoire de l'amante invisible".

Why this triumph? Because the story represents not only the attitudes found in the novels of the time, but also a prevalent

---

[46] Scarron, *op. cit.,* p. 563.
[47] *Ibid.,* p. 564.
[48] Paul Scarron, *Roman comique,* Félix Guirard and André V. Pierre, éd. (Paris: Librairie Larousse, 1935), p. 8.
[49] Scarron, *op. cit.,* p. 551.
[50] *Ibid.,* p. 552.

attitude found in the bourgeoisie. Ragotin is the example of the bourgeois who redas novels and has literary ambitions. He is even similar to M. Jourdain. Ragotin is also a man deceived by the ideas in the novels like Don Quijote.

Chapter eleven in the *Roman comique* clarifies Ragotin's attitude. Ragotin and La Rancune go to the tripot where they proceed to drink. The following then transpires:

> La Rancune lui demanda ce qu'il disoit de leurs Comediennes. Le petit bonhomme rougit sans luy répondre. Et, la Rancune lui demandant encore la mesme chose, enfin begayant, rougissant et s'exprimant tres mal, il fit entendre a la Rancune qu'une des Comediennes lui plaisoit infiniment. Et laquelle? (lui dit la Rancune). Le petit homme estoit si troublé d'en avoir tant dit qu'il répondit: Je ne sçay. Ni moy aussy, dit la Rancune. Cela le troubla encore davantage et lui fit ajouter tout interdit: C'est... c'est... Il repeta quatre ou cinq fois le mesme mot dont le Comedien, s'impatientant, lui dit: Vous avez raison; c'est une fort belle fille. Cela acheva de le deffaire. Il ne put jamais dire celle à qui il en vouloit, et peut-estre qu'il n'en sçavoit rien encore et qu'il avoit moins d'amour que de vice. Enfin, la Rancune lui nommant Mademoiselle de l'Estoile, il dit que c'estoit elle dont il estoit amoureux; et, pourmoy, je croy que, s'il lui eust nommé Angelique ou sa mere la Caverne, qu'il eust oublie le coup busc de l'une et l'age de l'autre et se seroit donne corps et ame à celle que la Rancune luy auroit nommée. [57]

This passage presents in a comical fashion the same attitude presented in the *nouvelle,* and the same attitude found in the novels of the time. Women were supreme in the seventeenth century: Astrée could banish Céladon with one word; Oriana's anger led Amadis to Peña Pobre; Emilie ordered Cinna to commit treason for her sake. Women were goddesses who were forever to be pleased and never argued with. Their motives could not be questioned. Thus, women were placed on the pedestal of a neoplatonic love. Men worshipped not these particular women, but the ideal that each represented. Complete obedience was required as in the novels of chivalry.

---

[51] *Ibid.,* p. 573.

The aristocracy knew that all this was a game and a convention. They knew that Astrée did not exist, but pretended that their lady was Astrée, while they pretended to act as Céladon. When the middle class tried to imitate this idea, all pretenses were dropped. They were serious. They had no means of coping with their own imaginations.

Ragotin wants to love. He wants to adore a deity, but he does not know which. He is not capable of selecting so that the selection has to be made for him. Carlos does not choose either. *L'amante invisible* makes the choice, and he is bound by it. The story consists in his proving to her that he is worthy of her, as she states in their first conversation at the *reja*. Porcia never has to prove anything.

Love, then, for the seventeenth century, is something imposed on men. Man has to prove himself worthy of it. Ragotin, like men, accepts the burden of love without question. He serves, but what he serves is not a real woman, but an ideal created by the imagination. Carlos, we must remember, loves Porcia without ever having seen her. His love for her is also one of imagination. Remember the warning: "Ne croyez pas vostre imagination aux dépens de vostre jugement." [52] The novels of the time, with the consequent supremacy of women, had created a disease of the imagination that the bourgeois could not cope with. Ragotin tried to improve his existence by becoming a literary man, but since he did not understand the convention of the time, he was trapped by the stimulus the *novelas* had on the imagination. Thus Scarron in presenting this *nouvelle* is showing the reader the character of Ragotin, and the nature of his "madness." He is also criticizing contemporary customs and literature which are the cause of the madness. It can be considered that the *nouvelle* of "L'amante invisible" is not just an interpolated story having nothing to do with the action of the novel. Instead, it is an objective correlative of the whole action since it satirizes literature and morals; and these are the main points of the novel.

But Ragotin is a complex character. He is more than just a caricature of a ridiculous middle class man. Like Scarron, he takes the *nouvelle* from a Spanish source without revealing this source. He is then discovered for doing this and ridiculed. Scarron will later

---

[52] *Ibid.*, p. 558.

be "discovered" by D'Ouville. And yet, if D'Ouville had read with care the *Roman comique,* he would have realized that such an attack on Scarron was not needed, since he had already done it through the character of Ragotin.

Scarron's foresight goes even farther. He has Ragotin state that he will write a play on the subject. Then, the other players give their opinion of such an attempt. This piece of literary criticism may seem unfounded. However, five years after the publication of the first part of the *Roman comique,* in 1656, a play appeared by Boisrobert called *Le belle invisible,* based on this short story. Thus, Scarron had ridiculed a play that did not come into being until five years later. [53]

Scarron in his adaptation of "Los efectos que hace amor" is able to criticize not only past and present literature, but also future literature. He satirizes customs, ideas, and people, and tries to have his contemporaries take heed of his sententious saying: "Ne croyez pas vostre imagination aux dépens de vostre jugement." [54]

---

[53] Scarron may have thought, however, that *La Jalouse d'elle mesme* (1650) by Boisrobert was an imitation of Castillo Solórzano and thus he may have been criticizing a play that had been produced the year before the publication of the *Roman comique.* This play is not based on Castillo Solórzano, but on Tirso de Molina's *La celosa de si misma.*

[54] *Ibid.,* p. 585.

Chapter III

A TROMPEUR, TROMPEUR ET DEMI

This chapter will discuss the second interporlated story in the first part of the *Roman comique* which appeared in 1651. It is told, appropriately, by a Spanish lady called Inezilla, and is preceeded by a discussion of what Scarron considered to be the merits of the Spanish *nouvelle*. Garouffière states:

> Que les Espagnols avoient le secret de faire de petites histoires, qu'ils appellent Nouvelles, qui sont bien plus a notre usage et plus selon la portée de l'humanité que ces Heros imaginaires de l'antiquité qui sont quelquefois incommodes à force d'estre trop honnestes gens. [1]

This story will be completely different from the previous one, since in the "Histoire de l'amante invisible" Scarron was trying to ridicule the novel and the heroes of novels, while here he is trying to show what a short piece of fiction should be like. It is interesting to note that this story, just as the previous one, is taken from Alonso de Castillo Solórzano.

Antoine Adam, G. Hainsworth, and other critics, state that this second interpolated story, "A trompeur, trompeur et demi," is taken from "A un engaño, otro mayor," the third story of *Los alivios de Casandra*. This seems to be true since the stories are very similar, the titles are the same, and it is taken from the same collection as the previous story. A comparison shows that the first half

---

[1] Paul Scarron, *Le Roman comique* in *Romanciers du XVIIe siècle*, Antoine Adam, éd. (Paris: Bibliothèque de la Pléiade, 1962), p. 645.

of each tale is almost identical; but at a certain point the French version deviates completely from the original.

R. Cadorel, in his work, *Scarron et la nouvelle espagnole dans le Roman comique,* states that the source of "A trompeur, trompeur et demi" is "A lo que obliga el honor," the third interpolated story in *La garduña de Sevilla,* a picaresque novel published by Castillo Solórzano two years after *Los alivios de Casandra.* A comparison of the two stories shows that while their beginnings differ a great deal, they are very similar in their conclusions. Thus, Scarron used the first half of "A un engaño, otro mayor," and the conclusion of "A lo que obliga el honor" when he composed his story "A trompeur, trompeur et demi."

First, "A un engaño, otro mayor" will be compared to Scarron's second interpolated story. As with the "Histoire de l'amante invisible," there are here many mechanical changes to make the story more palatable to the French audience, who are imbued with more classical ideas.

Straightforwardness is a characteristic very much appreciated by Scarron and the classicists. For example, when a man is brought in to Victorias' presence he is immediately identified in Scarron as Dom Lopes de Gongora.[2] In Castillo Solórzano, he is not mentioned by name until after Victoria has fallen in love with him.[3]

Also, when Victoria finds the letter wrapped around a portrait and reads it, a compliment is paid in the letter to the lady of the portrait in two different manners. Castillo Solórzano is more "poetic," while Scarron is more prosaic.

Castillo Solórzano adds an unnecessary complication when he has Victoria change her name to Teodora as she enters Blanca de la Cerda's service.[4] In Scarron no such change occurs. There is justification for the change of name in Castillo Solórzano since this way she will be harder to detect by Don Fernando. However, added names create confusion, and Scarron, by avoiding this detail, makes his story easier to read.

---

[2] *Ibid.,* p. 647.
[3] Alonso de Castillo Solórzano, *Los alivios de Casandra* (Barcelona: Imprenta de Jayme Romeu, 1640), p. 44.
[4] *Ibid.,* p. 48.

Another example of how Scarron re-arranged the Spanish *novela* to create a straightforward plot is seen when Feliciano goes to Don Pedro de Silva's house to offer his daughter as a *Duegna* to Blanca. Two meetings are required in Castillo Solórzano. The first time Feliciano comes alone, while the second time he brings his daughter. Scarron does not see the need for two meetings and has the servant and Victoria appear together at Don Pedro's house.

Scarron, to add to the smoothness and straightforwardness of the story, sometimes changes a *récit* from the first to the third person. This adds also to the conciseness of the story, and removes it from the long *récits* found in the novels; it must be remembered that Scarron is presenting this story as a contrast to the *romans héroïques*. An example of this is the *récit* of the feigned Dom Lopes de Gongora. The off-hand attitude of Scarron should be noticed. It makes the story more informal and more conversational, while the Spanish story remains rigid. Changes in detail will be discussed later. Here are both versions:

> Mi patria es Cordova, mi prosapia noble, pues es de los Gongoras de aquella Ciudad, cavalleros muy conocidos en ella; parti de alli con alguna priessa a la Corte por hallarme a la sentencia de un pleyto de consideracion que traygo con un cavallero muy poderoso, y para que me tuviessen prevenida posada en Toledo, embiè delante desde Orgaz al moço de mulas que me venia sirviendo, tomando relacion del camino hasta Toledo; sali algo tarde por temer los rigores del calor, y con la noche erramos el camino, en ocasion que no hallamos a quien preguntar por el, dando con nuestras mulas en unos olivares donde en lo espesso dellos nos acabamos de perder del todo; visto esto me parecio mas a proposito apearnos antes que caminar toda la noche a ciegas, desviandonos del camino principal, y assi lo hize, queriendo passar alli la noche, hasta que con la luz del alba hallasemos el camino, o quien nos guiasse a el, tendimos el rancho en los coxines, atando las mulas a los arboles, donde seguros de lo que nos sucedio, nos entregamos con descuydo al sueño q̃ como ladron de los sentidos vino llamando del cansancio; en este sossiego estabamos los dos, quando nos despertò el susto de vernos abraçados de unos hombres, que en el mesmo serian hasta quatro, los quales atandonos fuertemente con cordeles que

> traian, nos quitaron quanto traiamos dejandome solo cô este jubon. [5]

> Luy dit qu'il estoit un Gentilhomme de Cordoüe appelé Dom Lopes de Gongora ; qu'il venoit de Seville et qu'allant à Madrid pour des affaires d'importance et s'estant amusé à jouer à une demy journée de Tolede, où il avoit disné le jour auparavant, que la nuict l'avoict surpris ; qu'il s'estoit endormy et son valet aussy en attendant un Mulletier qui estoit demeuré derriere ; et que des voleurs, l'ayans trouvé comme il dormoit, l'avoient lié à un arbre, et son valet aussy, après les avoir despouillez jusqu'à la chemise. [6]

In addition to smoothness, informality and straight-forwardness, Scarron changes the rambling Spanish story by eliminating what he considers to be needless detail. Notice above how Scarron does not mention that the thieves tied them strongly with a rope or that they were four in number. He does not state either that they lost their way, only that night came.

Scarron, in his story, never mentions that the reason why Victoria's brother is fighting in the low countries is that he killed a man:

> Obligavala a estar alli la ausencia de un hermano suyo, que por la muerte hizo de un cavallero, se havia ydo a Flandes, donde militava en los exercitos del Rey de España contra los Olandeses. [7]

This Scarron considers irrelevant to the story, while Castillo Solórzano not only states it at the beginning of the story, but later has Victoria describe all the details:

> Quedè en el amparo de don Bernardino mi hermano a quien honra el pecho la roja Cruz de Santiago, como la juventud en los cavalleros de la edad de don Bernardino, siempre les inclina a exercicios de moços, entre algunos a que se inclino fue uno al juego cosa tan dañosa en todos estados, pues solo sirve de ser polilla de la haziendas y de las honras pues quien es tahur està sujeto a la necesitad

---

[5] *Ibid.*, pp. 42-43.
[6] Scarron, *op. cit.*, pp. 647-648.
[7] Castillo Solórzano, *op. cit.*, p. 41.

y a sufrir en el juego, que se le iguale el plebeyo, con otras
cosas q̄ callo, y vos mejor lo sabreys, aunque no sea por
experiencia. Un dia de los que assistia jugando, tuvo pala-
bras con otro cavallero, de donde se originò el, que des-
mintiesse a mi hermano, obligandole esto a sacar una daga,
y matarle con tres puñaladas que le dio. Retirose a un
Convento, teniendo el rigor de la justicia, q̄ en Castilla es
mas severa que en otras partes, fue buscado en su casa,
embargaronle los muebles della, y parte dellos se vendieron
para despachar requisitorias, que le buscassen y pren-
diessen; mas el se puso a salvo con ausentarse de España,
yendose a Flandes. [8]

At the beginning of the story, Scarron attributes several good qualities to Victoria which should be mentioned. The story will not show them by example. There are some other qualities such as compassion, which will be shown through examples and need not be mentioned, so they are not. Castillo Solórzano not only gives examples but also tells us what they mean. When Victoria clothes Dom Lopes the reader is told that she does it because of compassion.[9] This is so obvious that Scarron deletes it, considering it a needless detail.

Other details are not only needless, but detract from the story. For example, when Dom Lopes is brought in we are told by Castillo Solórzano that he was "no poco corrido de verse assi desnudo."[10] This is completely irrelevant, and may even go against French *bienséance*. Also in violation of *bienséance* may be the fact that Victoria hides and looks at Dom Lopes after he has put on the clothes she has given him:

> Y assi (quitando los habitos dellos) se los vistieron, y les
> vinieron bien, mucho se holgo Victoria de ver el cavallero
> vestido, que assi manifestava mejor su buen talle, y ayrosa
> persona, y mirandole desde un retiro en que no podia ser
> vista se le aficiono. [11]

---

[8] *Ibid.*, pp. 54-55.
[9] *Ibid.*, p. 42.
[10] *Ibid.*
[11] *Ibid.*, p. 43.

In addition to the elimination of needless detail, Scarron also summarizes long and needless passages in the Spanish story, to add the conciseness of the French version. When Dom Lopes walks in, Victoria immediately realizes that he is of genteel birth. It takes Scarron two lines to state this, while Castillo Solórzano takes longer:

> Era Victoria compassiva, y assi acabada de vestir mandò a los forasteros que subiessen a su precencia, ellos lo hizieron, viendo la dama, un hombre de gentil talle, hermoso de rostro, proporcionado de miembros, bien compuesta barba, y bigotes, que solo su presencia manifestava aver en la nobleza.[12]

> La pauvreté de leur habit ne luy cacha point la riche mine du plus jeune, qui lui fit un complimen en honneste homme.[13]

A final example of conciseness is noted when Dom Lopes leaves Victoria to go to Madrid and he falls from his mule. In the Spanish version there is a long digression on the role of the servant. This entire aside is lacking in Scarron who does not even mention Dom Lopes' servant:

> Reprehendiale su criado el aver tenido tan grande atrevimiento con una señora, que le constaba ser noble, y de lo mas estimado de Toledo, de lo qual no le podia resultar ningun bien antes mucha inquietud, a saber que avía sido burlada.... Enoxose desto don Fernando, y mandole que en aquella platica no le hablasse mas pena de que le costaría caro hazerlo, con que el buen sirviente puso en silencio sus reprehensiones, y trató de adular a su señor.[14]

Not only does Scarron eliminate needless detail, summarize long passages, and delete digression, but he also eliminates all the figures of speech given by Castillo Solórzano, and there are several of these. For example, in discussing how the *cigarrales* of Victoria near Toledo are watered by the river Tajo, Castillo Solórzano states: "A quien

---

[12] *Ibid.*, p. 42.
[13] Scarron, *op. cit.*, p. 647.
[14] Castillo Solórzano, *op. cit.*, p. 47.

el dorado Taxo fecundava con sus cristales." [15] Compare this to Scarron's flat statement: "Une maison qu'elle avoit sur les bords du Tage." [16]

When Dom Lopes goes to sleep, Scarron states simply: "qu'il s'estoit endormy et son valet aussy," [17] while Castillo Solórzano must embellish every action: "Nos entregamos con descuydo al sueño q̄ como ladron de los sentidos vino llamado del cansancio." [18] Even when Victoria cries, Castillo Solórzano, contrary to Scarron's procedure, must state this with a metaphor: "Hecha un mar de lagrimas." [19]

This desire for adornment runs contrary to Scarron's purpose, which is to present a simple veritable narrative that would contrast with the elaborateness of the *roman héroïque,* but would at the same time retain the interest of the reader. Scarron, in fact, states:

> Si l'on faisoit des Nouvelles en François, aussy bien faites que quelques-unes de celles de Michel de Cervantes, elles auroient cours autant que les Romans Héroïques. [20]

Scarron also likes to eliminate all sententious sayings or maxims from his work. He places them in the same plane as the metaphor, even if a Corneille used them sparingly, and Mme de Sevigné praised him for it. Such sententious sayings are meant for a more serious style. A *nouvelle* does not share the stated didacticism of the stage. Scarron changes Castillo Solórzano's style in that he considers that a *nouvelle* can only instruct through implication since its style is directed toward entertainment, while the Spanish author must make obvious his didacticisms by direct statement.

A list of some of the sayings which Scarron deleted follows. When Dom Lopes is trying to seduce Victoria, he flatters her because, as Castillo Solórzano declares, "La introduccion del amor comiença por la alabança, y esta es creida de todas las mugeres." [21]

---

[15] *Ibid.,* p. 41.
[16] Scarron, *op. cit.,* p. 647.
[17] *Ibid.*
[18] Castillo Solórzano, *op. cit.,* p. 43.
[19] *Ibid.,* p. 45.
[20] Scarron, *op. cit.,* p. 645.
[21] Castillo Solórzano, *op. cit.,* p. 44.

Another comment by Castillo Solórzano on love occurs when, after only a few days, Victoria gives in to Dom Lopes. This, the Spanish author states, was the downfall of Victoria: "Porque todo lo que mucho cuesta en las pretensiones amorosas, es de mayor estimacion, y se desea mas." [22]

This impetuousness on her part is essential to the story and will be discussed later. Jealously, according to Castillo Solórzano, is an essential part of passion. Thus he also present a reflection on it: "Los mismos celos (como antojos) aumentan las cosas mas de lo que son." [23]

The Spanish author does not stop with abstractions. He also gives us reflections on practical things as customs of the time:

> Y tratò de adular a su señor, pues en esso consistia su medra, calamidad de estos tiempos aun en mas altos personajes, que no se atreven a hablar libre contra los poderosos por sus particulares interesses. [24]

Sometimes these sententious sayings verge on the cynical. When Dom Lopes leaves Victoria, the Spanish author tells the reader he will forget her because: "En los hombres es muy ordinario tener en menos lo que es gozado." [25]

All these general statements on behavior are absent in Scarron. However, there is in Scarron a tendency to generalize as opposed to the specific details of the Spanish author. This is so when moral questions are not involved, and especially when these details are not familiar to a French audience. In the Spanish version, Dom Lopes is tied to an olive tree by the thieves. [26] Scarron only states that he is tied to a tree. [27] It is not necessary for the reader to know what kind of tree it is; all that matters is that a tree was there.

When Feliciano makes up a story to tell Dom Pedro, he states in the Spanish version that he comes from Carmona. [28] This name is

---

[22] *Ibid.*
[23] *Ibid.*, p. 45.
[24] *Ibid.*, p. 47.
[25] *Ibid.*, p. 45.
[26] *Ibid.*, p. 42.
[27] Scarron, *op. cit.*, p. 647.
[28] Castillo Solórzano, *op. cit.*, p. 48.

totally unfamiliar to the French. Scarron makes it more general: "Un pauvre Gentil-homme des montagnes de Tolede." [29]

All the changes mentioned thus far have to do with the simplification and clarification of the more ornate Spanish style. Additions are also made by Scarron.

First of all, as in the "Histoire de l'amante invisible," Scarron introduces humor into the story. When Victoria reads the letter attached to the portrait she begins to cry and faints in the Spanish version. This is all described with great seriousness. Scarron tries to lighten the tale here, in keeping with the character of a *nouvelle*:

> Jamais personne ne s'affligea tant; ses soupirs la penserent suffoquer et elle pleura jusqu'à s'en faire mal à la teste. [30]

What is most significant in this story concerning humor is its absence and not its presence; even G. Hainsworth notes this. [31] This is in sharp contrast with the first interporlated story. Scarron was ridiculing in the first story the heroic novel and its heroes. This second *nouvelle* is not intended as a model of what one should not do but of what one should do. Thus, he will not use humor or satire. It should be pleasant and light but not satirical. Inezilla's story is to be taken seriously, while Ragotin's is to be taken lightly, as is everything he does. Inezilla is not raeding out someone else's story in order to gain fame. She is trying to become a writer like her former husband. As stated in the previous chapter of the *Roman comique*, a Spanish *nouvelle* modeled after Cervantes can succeed as well as a heroic novel.

In addition to a very few instances of humor, Scarron adds explanations where he thinks there might be some reason for confusion. After Victoria reads the letter attached to the portrait she realizes that Dom Lopes is really Dom Fernand. This is obvious to any reader and Castillo Solórzano does not attempt to add any explanation. Scarron on the other hand adds a lengthy explanation of the reason for the change of names. Later he does not change

---

[29] Scarron, *op. cit.*, p. 651.
[30] *Ibid.*, p. 649.
[31] G. Hainsworth, *Les "Nouvelles Exemplaires" de Cervantes en France au XVII*e *siècle* (Paris: Librairie Ancienne Honoré Champion, 1933), p. 102.

the name of Victoria to Teodora either. This great care to explain people's names may derive from his desire for clarity. Yet, the following explanation which he includes is superfluous:

> La lettre s'addressoit à Fernand de Ribera, à Seville. Representez-vous, je vous prie, l'estonnement de Victoria à la lecture d'une telle lettre qui, selon toutes les apparences du monde, ne pouvoit estre escrite à un autre qu'à son Lopes de Gongora. Elle voyoit, mais trop tard, que cet étranger qu'elle avoit si fort obligé, et si viste, luy avoit deguisé son nom et, par ce déguisement-là, elle devoit estre asseurée de son infidelité. [32]

Other explanations given by Scarron are more to the point. Castillo Solórzano states that when Dom Fernand leaves Victoria to go to Madrid, his mule throws him. No reason is given except that this is the beginning of God's punishment. Scarron tries to give a more practical interpretation, since the reader might think that being robbed and then being thrown from a horse might be too many misfortunes in too short a time. Here are both versions, showing Scarron's explanation:

> A don Fernando se le espantò la mula en q̄ iva, de modo que congiendole descuydado dio con el en el suelo una caida tal, que le sacò un braço de su lugar, ya començava el cielo a castigar su delito. [33]

> Le jour mesme qu'il partit de chez Victoria, Dieu le punit de sa perfidie. En arrivant a Illescas, un chien, qui sortit d'une maison à l'improviste, fit peur à son mulet qui luy froissa une jambe contre une muraille et le jetta par terre. [34]

In addition to these purely mechanical explanations, Scarron adds some that try to exploit the seventeenth century reader's curiosity about Spanish customs. He adds local color whenever he can. When Victoria gives the pretended Dom Lopes clothes to wear that used to belong to her brother, Scarron gives an explanation as to why the

---

[32] Scarron, *op. cit.*, p. 649.
[33] Castillo Solórzano, *op. cit.*, p. 47.
[34] Scarron, *op. cit.*, p. 652.

clothes were there, while Castillo Solórzano tells the reader what these clothes were:

> De alli a un rato la vio salir acompañada de dos criadas suyas, las quales venian con dos vestidos embueltos en dos toallas, estos ofrecio al forastero para el, y su criado, pidiendole muchos perdones de que no fuessen nuevos, pero assegurandole avia muy poco que se avian hecho, y que eran de un hermano suyo, cuya calidad vieron en las ropillas por tener la roja Cruz del patron de España, eran los vestidos negros, porque don Gonçalo Portocarrero hermano desta dama, dejò un baul de vestidos en su poder quando se partio a Flandes.[35]

> Il se rencontra heureusement que, parmy les hardes que son frère luy avoit laissées en garde, il y avoit quelques habits; car les Espagnols ne quittent point leurs vieux habits pour jamais, quand ils en prennent des neufs.[36]

There are some changes in addition to the ones already stated that Scarron made to "A un engaño, otro mayor," and that should be discussed. Scarron states that the reason why Dom Lopes was delayed and that night fell before he arrived in Toledo was that he had been gambling: "Et s'estant amusé à jouer à une demy journée de Tolède..."[37] In "A un engaño, otro mayor" the reason given was that he was trying to avoid the warm weather. However, in "A lo que obliga el honor" the reason for the delay was also gambling:

> El se quedó entreteniendo sombremesa con unos hidalgos de Orgaz —que era el lugar donde estaba— a los naipes; perdía y picóse, con que el juego duró hasta que le dieron lugar a desquitarse, que fué algo más tarde que quisiera.[38]

The question then is why Scarron used this detail from the 1642 story while taking the rest of the first half of his *nouvelle* from the 1640 story. Gambling shows impetuousness, and this is the main

---

[35] Castillo Solórzano, *op. cit.*, p. 43.
[36] Scarron, *op. cit.*, p. 648.
[37] *Ibid.*, p. 647.
[38] Alonso de Castillo Solórzano, *La garduña de Sevilla* (Madrid: "Ediciones de "La Lectura," 1922), p. 261.

point of the story, as will be seen later. Thus, the change is made to further emphasize the main theme.

Other small changes are there to increase the verisimilitude of the story. Dom Lopes' seduction of Victoria takes very fow days in Castillo Solórzano. Scarron thinks that ot seduce a lady as virtuous as Victoria, Dom Lopes need at least fifteen days, so the time is extended. It should be recalled that time was also extended in the "Histoire de L'Amante Invisible."

When Victoria leaves for Madrid, Castillo Solórzano implies that she does not care what people might think of her sudden departure. This is frowned on by Scarron who wants to preserve the image of Victoria, since he is not so much concerned with her honor, which is an interior quality most prized by the Spanish, but with other people's opinions. Thus he devises an excuse:

> Et Victoria, faisant courir le bruit parmy ses domestiques qu'il falloit qu'elle allast à la Cour pour les affaires pressantes de son frère, elle monta en carosse avec son Escuyer et sa Suivante, prit le chemin de Madrid et se fit suivre par son bagage. [39]

When Dom Lopes leaves Victoria, there is a clear statement in Castillo Solórzano that he did not care for her, since he left "fingiendo de mas a mas lagrimas y sentimiento." [40] Scarron leaves this point ambiguous for two reasons. Victoria will have to marry him in the end, and he must not appear totally uncorcerned. Second, he is not pictured in Scarron as being evil, but just impetuous. This is what Scarron states:

> La pauvre Dame veritablement accablée de douleur quand il partit, et luy, s'il ne fut pas beaucoup affligé, le contrefaisant avec la plus grande hypocrisie du monde. [41]

There are some other changes by Scarron that may proceed from the fact that he did not remember what the Spanish version stated or that he misunderstood. Scarron states in his description of Victoria that she is a widow:

---

[39] Scarron, *op. cit.*, p. 650.
[40] Castillo Solórzano, *Los alivios de Casandra*, p. 45.
[41] Scarron, *op. cit.*, p. 649.

> Elle estoit demeurée veufve a l'âge de dix-sept ans, d'un vieil Gentilhomme qui s'estoit enrichy aux Indes et qui, s'estant perdu en mer six mois apres son mariage, avoit laissé beaucoup de biens a sa femme. [42]

This fact is nowhere to be found in either one of the Spanish stories. What does happen is that in the tale that Feliciano makes up about his pretended daughter Victoria (Teodora), is that she is a widow who in fact lost her husband at sea when he was returning with all his gold from the New World:

> Casé en aquella Ciudad una hija que tengo con un hidalgo honrado, que tratava en Indias, hizo un viaje al Piru, y a la buelta viniendo muy ganancioso de su empleo, la fortuna q̄ nunca tiene permanencia en nada, le anegò el galeon en que traia todo su caudal, pereciendo con el en el mar. [43]

This may be a misunderstanding on Scarron's part or it may be that since he was not going to give a long *récit* about Teodora, he wanted to include the story of a shipwreck somewhere, since they were so popular during his time. However, knowing that he disliked unnecessary or irrelevant details, and knowing that he satirized the contemporary novel, this may seem unlikely.

Scarron again seems to misunderstand Castillo Solórzano when he tries to explain why Dom Lopes did not have his muleteer when the thieves found him. In Scarron the muleteer had remained behind, while in Castillo Solórzano he had gone ahead:

> Y para que me tuviessen prevenida posada en Toledo, embie delante desde Orgaz al moço de mulas que me venia sirviendo. [44]

> Et attendant un Mulletier qui estoit demeure derriere. [45]

Also, Scarron did not seem to realize the importance of a detail in the Spanish story. The reason why Victoria gave in to Dom Lopes was because he promised to marry her. These false promises of

---
[42] *Ibid.*, p. 647.
[43] Castillo Solórzano, *Los alivios de Casandra*, p. 48.
[44] *Ibid.*, p. 42.
[45] Scarron, *op. cit.*, p. 648.

marriage are crucial in many Spanish *novelas*. In *Don Quijote de la Mancha* for example Dorotea gives in to Fernando (notice the similarity or names) because he verbally promises to marry her. When she realizes that he was only deceiving her, she leaves her home disguised and tries to find Fernando and prevent him from getting married to another beautiful lady. Again, notice the similarity of plot. Here is what Castillo Solórzano states:

> Hallo en Victoria resistencia su desseo, sino la tuvo en ocultar su amor, y assi le dijo, que menos de que la diesse palabra de esposo con cedula suya firmada en que lo confessasse, no la tomaria una mano, estava aficionado della, y encendido en desseos, y determinose a darla gusto, si bien llevando adelante su engaño, porque la relacion que la avia hecho de patria y nombre era fingida. [46]

Thus, this deception is what triggered her fault. Scarron only attributes it to her love for him, nad belittles the promise of marriage:

> Enfin, en quinze jours, la commodité du lieu, le merite egal en ces deux jeunes personnes, quantité de sermens d'un costé, trop de franchise et de credulité de l'autre, une promesse de mariage offerte et la foy reciproquement donnée en presence d'un vieil Escuyer et d'une suivante de Victoria, luy firent faire une faute dont jamais on ne l'eust crû capable et mirent ce bienheureux estranger en possession de la plus belle Dame de Tolede. [47]

This may not necessarily be a misinterpretation. The Spanish story deals with honor, and how it must be recovered. There would be no honor to recover if that promise had not been made. In Scarron, the main theme is not honor, but what impetuous actions can cause. Thus, Scarron is following his main idea when he disregards such a crucial point.

There are several other changes of detail in the French version that serve to change completely the picture of Victoria. As in the "Histoire de l'amante invisible," women are the center of the action.

---

[46] Castillo Solórzano, *Los alivios de Casandra*, p. 44.
[47] Scarron, *op. cit.*, p. 648.

Porcia had decided that she would marry Dom Carlos after he proved himself worthy, and she did. Now, Victoria decides that she must marry Dom Fernand in order to atone for her impetuousness. It is her will power and resourcefullness that brings about the marriage. Men in these stories obey the will of their mistresses in the end.

In Castillo Solórzano, Victoria is seen as a weak woman. Scarron will change this by changing several events. First, when Victoria finds out that Dom Fernand has deceived her, that his name is not Dom Lope de Gongora, and that he does not intend to marry her but another lady in Madrid, she fainst in the Spanish version. She is stronger in the French version where, as stated before, she cries "jusqu'a s'en faire mal à la teste." [48]

Following this, Victoria reproaches Dom Fernand in the Spanish version, while in the French story she has enough fortitude to realize that it is also her fault. Here are both versions:

> A quanto a dañado a las mugeres nuestra facilidad en creer, y nuestra determinacion en obrar! quien creyera que en sangre noble cupiera tan infame trato? tan vil correspondencia, y tan grande arrojamiento? q̄ podrà hazer una muger flaca sola, y sin amparo? quando me quiera valer de mis deudos ellos me han de menospreciar, sabiendo lo que he hecho. [49]

> Miserable que je suis! disoit-elle quelquefois en elle mesme et quelquefois aussy devant son vieil Escuyer et sa suivante que avoient esté témoins de son Mariage, ay-je esté si long-temps sage pour faire une faute irreparable et devois-je refuser tant de personnes de condition de ma connoissance, qui se fussent estimées heureuses de me posseder, pour me donner à un Inconnu qui se mocque peut-estre de moy après m'avoir rendue malheureuse pour toute ma vie? ....Que ne fera point mon frere contre moi, après ce que j'ay fait moy-mesme et de quoy luy sert l'honneur qu'il acquiert en Flandre tandis que je le deshonore en Espagne? [50]

---

[48] *Ibid.*, p. 649.
[49] Castillo Solórzano, *Los alivios de Casandra*, p. 46.
[50] Scarron, *op. cit.*, p. 650.

The use of the word honor in Scarron is not the same as in the Spanish version, since for Scarron in the passage above, honor is more public opinion than a virtue. Then, in the Spanish version, Victoria utters threats: she will kill the deceiver and avenge her honor. She is almost hysterical. The French version, on the other hand, shows a Victoria with great self-control and in full possession of her powers of reasoning. It is as if Scarron, in rewriting this story, wanted to remind the reader of the key point of the first interpolated story: judgment. Victoria, in her burning passion ("Ce ne fut que de feu et de flammes") [51] had given vent to her imagination and believed in Dom Fernand's pure and eternal love. Now, faced with reality, her judgment was returned, and she was able to consider calmly ways of amending her mistake. Here are both versions:

> Sino a tratar de mi vengança por el camino que pueda guardate falso engañador de una muger ofendida, y agraviada de tu proceder, que esta alevosia te a de costar no menos que la vida. [52]

> Non, non, Victoria, il faut tout entreprendre puisque nous avons tout oublié; mais, devant que d'en venir à la vengeance et aux derniers remedes, il faut essayer de gagner par adresse ce que nous avons mal conserve par imprudence. Il sera tousjours assez à temps de se perdre quand il n'y aura plus rien a esperer. [53]

The hysterical threats of a weak Victoria that has been put to bed by her servants are only quietud in the Spanish version when Feliciano, an old servant who has raised Victoria and her brother, comes to see her and counsels her. This servant is then the voice of reason in the Spanish version, while no such person counsels her in Scarron:

> Estas razones dezia la violada Victoria, estava oyendo Feliciano criado anciano de su casa a quien las dos criadas avian llamado, y dado quēta de la pena en que su señora

---

[51] *Ibid.*, p. 648.
[52] Castillo Solórzano, *Los alivios de Casandra*, p. 46.
[53] Scarron, *op. cit.*, p. 650.

> estava; este como oyesse quejarse a la afligida dama de ser engañada del forastero, entrò en su aposento, y descançando con el Victoria le diò quenta de todo lo sucedido sin reservarle nada, el buen viejo avia muchos años que servia en su casa, y avia criado a Victoria y a su ausente hermano, y querialos tan tiernamente que no llegara a mas quilates su amor si fueran hijos suyos, y assi doliendose de lo que Victoria le requeria, la aconsejò. [54]

Not only does Feliciano counsel Victoria at this point in the Spanish version, but she also obeys him as a father throughout the *novela*. This obedience again detracts from the judgment and will power of Victoria in the Spanish version so Scarron does not mention it. Here is what Castillo Solórzano states when Victoria and Feliciano arrive in Madrid: "Dispuesta la dama a obedecerle en todo como padre." [55] No mention of this is found in the French story.

Victoria is a different woman in Scarron, just as Dom Fernand is a different man, since he is the impetuous man and not the evil man found in Castillo Solórzano. In addition to a change in character, we find in Scarron several other changes that modify the tone of the *novela*. Scarron improves the Spanish story be eliminating anticipation. It is a very common element in Castillo Solórzano to find him stating what is going to happen later in the story. Scarron tries to keep the reader in suspense.

When Victoria falls in love with Dom Lopes (Fernand), Castillo Solórzano warns: "De manera que le costó el amoroso tiro (que entonces hizo el amor) muchas penas, como después sabreys." [56] Before the servant finds the letter which proves to Victoria that Dom Fernand is deceiving her, Castillo Solórzano states: "La relacion que la avia hecho de patria, y nombre era fingida." [57] He even states: "Porque... le esperaba otra belleza en Madrid." [58] Thus, the surprise of the letter is not present in Castillo Solórzano as it is in Scarron. These changes create a story where the interest is sustained throughout.

---

[54] Castillo Solórzano, *Los alivios de Casandra*, p. 46.
[55] *Ibid.*, p. 48.
[56] *Ibid.*, p. 43.
[57] *Ibid.*, p. 44.
[58] *Ibid.*

There is, however, one change in structure which does not seem appropriate. In Castillo Solórzano, as soon as Victoria and Feliciano arrive in Madrid, the old servant goes out to try to determine what happened to Dom Fernand. He does, and his delay, caused by a broken arm, inspires the old servant to have Victoria enter as a *dueña* to doña Blanca (Elvire) and try to undermine the marriage:

> Todo esto vino a saber el anciano hayo de doña Victoria, que hazia diligencias para informarse con certeza de no aver llegado a Madrid con lo qual se animo a emprender una linda quimera, que fue el total rememdio de Victoria, comunicolo con ella. [59]

Scarron does not tell the reader what happened to Dom Fernand until after Victoria has been hired as a *dueña* to doña Blanca. Thus, she entered Elvire's service without knowing of Dom Fernand's delay. This creates a lack of motivation in the story, since if she did not know that Dom Fernand was not in town, she could not have conceived the idea of undermining the marriage before he arrived. It is at this point, when Dom Fernand comes back to Madrid, that Scarron changes texts.

Scarron the changed "A un engaño, otro mayor" mainly through the change of character in both Victoria and Dom Fernand. The Spanish version deals with honor and duty. Scarron, firmly believing that a *nouvelle* should have a lighter tone, discusses exactly the same thing he presented in the first story: lack of judgment. To do this, he must make Fernand into an impetuous and unthinking man. Thus, he adds that he had been gambling and he does not firmly state that his feelings for Victoria were counterfeit. In addition Scarron talks of the burning passion of the two lovers. Thus, his action was impetuous and not premeditated deception. Castillo Solórzano can afford to make Fernand into an evil person since later on in "A un engaño, otro mayor," he will fight a duel where he will demonstrate his courage. This duel, however, is not present in "A lo que obliga el honor" or in Scarron's tale.

---

[59] *Ibid.*, p. 48.

Victoria emerges as a woman of self-confidence, will power and judgment. She knows what she must do and tries to find the means through action, while the Victoria of Castillo Solórzano would have remained in bed uttering empty threats if it had not been for Feliciano. Scarron, in contrast to Castillo Solórzano, states flatly: "Victoria avoit l'esprit bien fort." [60]

Scarron did not use "A lo que obliga el honor" for the first part of the story. A brief analysis of the structure will show this. The third interpolated story in *La garduña de Sevilla* begins with the birth of Fernand. It tells of his youth and how he had a cousin in Madrid who had a friend whose daughter needed a husband. Portraits are exchanged, and Fernand sets out for Madrid. On his trip, he is caught by thieves just outside Toledo and is rescued the next day by shepherds who take him to Victoria's home. The affair with Victoria is very briefly described, and then he sets out for Madrid, on the way falling and breaking his leg. The fact that he breaks his leg and not his arm is one detail the French author took from the first part of this *novela*. "A lo que obliga el honor" then reverts to Toledo where Victoria finds the letter and is counseled by her servant to set out for Madrid, where she becomes a *dueña to* doña Blanca. As can be seen, the structure of this second story is completely different. The question may be raised as to why Scarron did not use the first half of this story. The answer may be that the structure is too simple. It takes place in almost chronological order. "A un engaño, otro mayor" begins *in medias res*. Its construction shows greater art since it begins at a point of great interest: when the shepherds bring in to Victoria's house an unknown man whom they have found tied to a tree. This type of beginning was common in the heroic novels of the time where the narrative usually begins at the point where the two lovers are about to get together, but are suddenly separated by a great catastrophe. The catastrophe in this story is not a shipwreck or an earthquake but a more *vraisemblable* event: the fact that Fernand is already engaged to another woman.

The 1640 story then proceeds with the man's deception. The reader is deceived as much as Victoria, and when she finds the letter, the reader is as surprised as she is. Thus, the element of

---

[60] Scarron, *op. cit.*, p. 650.

surprise exists in "A un engaño, otro mayor," while it is lacking in "A lo que obliga el honor." Scarron was very conscious of this element as noted when he eliminated the anticipations present in Castillo Solórzano. This element of surprise was also present in the "Histoire de l'amante invisible," where the reader was as surprised as Dom Carlos to find that Porcia and the invisible lady were one and the same.

From this point on, Scarron follows almost word for word the 1642 version which has a completely different ending from the first story. Here is how "A un engaño, otro mayor" continues: Fernand comes back, Victoria tells Blanca that night of a Brianda Tenorio, a lady in Sevilla who has promise of marriage from Dom Fernand. The next day Victoria deceives a servant into giving her all of Dom Fernand's letters. She inserts one she wrote signed Brianda Tenorio and takes the letters to her mistress asking for Fernand. Blanca, very curious after Victoria's revelation, opens a letter that appears to be written by a woman and finds that it is from Brianda Tenorio.

Doña Blanca then tells Dom Fernand that she hates him, while he tries to get her back through the *dueña,* Victoria, whom he has not recognized. He even signs a blank piece of paper to her on which she has Feliciano write a promise of marriage. Dressed up as a lady, she then meets with Blanca's father, Don Pedro de la Cerda, and shows him Fernand's promise of marriage.

The father confronts Dom Fernand and his brother with the promise of marriage. At this time, don Bernardino, Victoria's brother, arrives, and finding out about Fernand, challenges him to a duel. They are both seriously wounded. The work ends with a double marriage: don Bernardino marries doña Blanca, while Fernand marries Victoria.

"A lo que obliga el honor" is totally different, since there, the brother never returns, there is no duel, and the dual marriage that occurs is between Dom Fernand and Victoria, and Doña Blanca and her secret lover. The only reason Blanca was going to marry Fernand in this story is because her father had ordered her to.

Thus far we have listed characters by their names in "A un engaño, otro mayor." The names are totally different in "A lo que obliga el honor." Scarron uses names from both stories and creates some of his own. The names also point to where Scarron left the first text and began using the second.

Victoria's family name in the 1640 Spanish version is Portocarrero. This is the same name used by Scarron. Dom Fernand's last name is Ribera in both versions. However, Blanca is named Elvire in Scarron and Brianda in the 1642 version. The name Elvira is found in the second Spanish version but it refers to the lady that Victoria invented from Sevilla. The name Brianda is found in the 1640 Spanish version and also refers to the Sevillan lady. Thus, twice the names of the Madrid lady are transferred ot the Sevillan lady. Scarron may have been aware of Castillo Solórzano's change and may have been pointing it out. He also may be pointing to the fact that both ladies have a similar role, although one is imagined: they both exist to prevent a marriage.

Blanca's family name in Scarron is Silva, while in the 1640 and 1642 Spanish versions it is Cerda. In "A lo que obliga el honor" the name Silva belongs to Victoria. Silva is a more common name, and was thus changed by Scarron. He may be also pointing out that Blanca is taking Victoria's rightful place, and must change her afections in the end. The family name of the Sevillan lady is Monsalve in both the French and the second Spanish version, while it is Tenorio in "A un engaño, otro mayor." Finally, Victoria's servant is called Rodrigue Santillane in Scarron, while he is Esteban de Santillana in the 1642 version. The name Santillana is the first use of a name from the 1642 text made by Scarron. It is used when they are already in Madrid and the servant is trying to have Victoria become Blanca's *dueña*. Thus, it occurs at about the time when Scarron changes texts. This may point to the fact that Scarron acquired the second text at this time, and did not know of it when he started the story.

However, if he did, it is to his credit, since by choosing for his first half "A un engaño, otro mayor," he chose the more artistic text as stated before. There are several other changes in names, but these will suffice as examples. Scarron was much closer to the text in the second half. The accuracy of detail points to the fact that he must have had the text in front of him and did not trust his memory. For example, in both texts Blanca reproaches Victoria for not flattering her on her choice of husband:

> Doña Teodora —que asi dijo llamarse—, ¿por qué cuando todas mis criadas me dan norabuenas de haber acertado

en la elección que he hecho para casarme, estás tú tan callada que, siquiera por lisonjearme, no la imitas? ¿De que nace tu silencio? [61]

Cependant Elvire demeura dans la chambre, environnée de toutes ses femmes qui se rejoüissoient devant elle de la bonne mine de son serviteur. La seule Victoria demeura froide et serieuse dans les emportemens des autres. Elvire le remarqua et la tira à part pour luy dire qu'elle s'estonnoit de ce qu'elle ne luy disoit rien de l'hereux choix que son pere avoit fait d'un Gendre qui paroissoit avoir tant de merite et ajousta qu'au moins, par flaterie ou par civilité, elle luy en devoit dire quelque chose. [62]

There are, however, some changes. When Victoria describes to Blanca's father the merits of her own father and brother, there is a slight change:

Mi padre y hermano, el uno tuvo el hábito de Santiago, y el otro tiene el de Alcántara. [63]

Mon pere portoit la croix de saint-Jacques et mon frere est de l'Ordre de Callatrava. [64]

In the Spanish version, Victoria is left with an old aunt after her father died and her brother went to war. This aunt died in a short while. The French version states that she was married but became a widow at sixteen:

Dejóme en Toledo en compañía de una tía anciana, que dentro de pocos días murió, y por su muerte me retiré a un cigarral que tengo cerca de Toledo. [65]

J'ay este mariée à seize ans et me suis trouvee veufve six mois aprés mon mariage. [66]

---

[61] Castillo Solórzano, *La garduña de Sevilla*, p. 270.
[62] Scarron, *op. cit.*, p. 653.
[63] Castillo Solórzano, *La garduña de Sevilla*, p. 280.
[64] Scarron, *op. cit.*, p. 659.
[65] Castillo Solórzano, *La garduña de Sevilla*, p. 281.
[66] Scarron, *op. cit.*, p. 659.

There is also in his part a tendency for Scarron to revert to the general when Castillo Solórzano is being specific. For example, when Castillo Solórzano states that Don Sancho (Diegue) was to arrive at eight, while Dom Fernand, at nine o'clock,[67] Scarron states that some time elapsed.[68]

There are also humorous additions as in the first part. As Elvire receives Dom Diegue, Scarron states:

> Je ne m'amuseray point à vous dire les carresses que ces jeunes Amans se firent. Dom Fernand qui frappe à la porte ne m'en donne pas le temps.[69]

If this statement is compared with the meeting of the lovers in the "Histoire de l'amante invisible," it becomes apparent that Scarron's humor is along the same lines:

> Ils se dirent encore cent belles choses, que je ne vous diray point, parce que je ne les sçay pas et que je n'ay garde de vous en composer d'autres de peur de faire tort a Dom Carlos et a la Dame Inconue, qui avoient bien plus d'esprit que j'en ay.[70]

There are also some changes, as in the first part, when Scarron believes that Castillo Solórzano is using too many words. Thus, the desire for conciseness is still present here. A more important question is why Scarron changed to this second story. The second part of this story is better constructed than the second part of the 1640 text. It is more concise, more interesting, and more straight-forward. One example of the three versions will suffice. Victoria now *dueña* of Blanca, will try to stop her marriage with Dom Fernand:

> Vino a ver a don Pedro el q̄ esperava ser presto novio de la belleza de Blanca, y ostentando su gala, y buen talle, don Pedro se pagó mucho del, y no menos Blanca, aquel dia (que todo fue de regozijo) en la casa de don Pedro) se hizieron las capitulaciones, entre suegro, y yerno, con mucha conformidad de los dos, según lo que tenia antes

---

[67] Castillo Solórzano, *La garduña de Sevilla*, p. 290.
[68] Scarron, *op. cit.*, p. 661.
[69] *Ibid.*, p. 662.
[70] *Ibid.*, p. 553.

tratado, y don Fernando estuvo muy fino con su esperada novia, todo aflicion y pena para Victoria, que como dueña de Blanca assistia junto a su estrado, y lo vía todo. Aquella noche retirada la novia a su quarto, trato con sus criadas de la buena dicha de su empleo, y quan acertado era, muy pagada de las partes del que esperava por dueño, aguardo Victoria (co lo que Feliciano la avía instruido) a que Blanca se quedase sola, y llegandose a ella, la dixo.... [71]

Estuvo el galán caballero muy gustoso en la visita y muy despejado, sin que se le pudiese notar la primera necedad de los novios, porque era don Pedro de claro entendimiento y de galan despejo. Vió el original de la hermosa Brianda haber andado fidelísimo el pincel, pocas veces usado a copiar verdades cuando se han de decir con los colores en empleos como éstos. Pagóse mucho de la hermosura de doña Brianda y ella le pagó en esto pues quedó muy contenta de la persona de don Pedro. Habíanse de asentar algunas cosas acerca deste casamiento que necesitaban de la persona de don Pedro, y así, él don Juan, y don Rodrigo se retiraron a otro cuarto, donde se encerraron con un escribano y algunos deudos que llamaron a hacer las capitulaciones; en tanto quedo doña Brianda con sus criadas tratando de la persona de don Pedro, su esperado esposo; todas la daban sus parabienes de que fuese tan a su gusto; solo Victoria no la decía nada, cosa que noto su señora; quedose a solas con ella y díjola: "Doña Teodora —que asi dijo llamarse— ¿por que cuando todas mis criadas me dan norabuenas de haber acertado en la elección que he hecho para casarme, estas tu tan callada que siquiera por lisonjearme, no la imitas? ¿De qué nace tu silencio? Había de propósito hecho aquello para venir despues a este lance como vino; vió la ocasion a medida de su deseo y quiso aprovecharse della, respondiendo a la propuesta doña Brianda asi: "Señora..." Alteróse con lo que oía doña Brianda, y con apretadas amonestaciones rogó a su dueña que le declarase lo oscuro de aquellas razones preñadas que no entendía. Ella, que se vio a rigor de derramar su ponzoña contra don Pedro, tirano de su honor, no fue perezosa en hacerlo, y así, pidiéndola que se fuesen a lugar menos registrado de sus criados y mas solo, se retiraron a un camarín donde la cauta Victoria dijo.... [72]

---

[71] Castillo Solórzano, *Los alivios de Casandra*, p. 49.
[72] Castillo Solórzano, *La garduña de Sevilla*, p. 271.

> Dom Fernand fut charmé de la beauté d'Elvire et advoua à son Cousin qu'elle estoit encore plus belle que son Portrait. Il luy fit ses premiers complimens en homme d'esprit et, parlant à elle et à son Pere, s'abstint le plus qu'il put de toutes les sottises que dit ordinairement, a un beaupere et à une Maistresse, un homme qui demande a se marier. Dom Pedro de Silva s'enferma dans un cabinet avec les deux cousins et avec un homme d'affaires pour ajouster quelque chose qui manquoit aux articles. Cependant Elvire demeura dans la chambre, environnée de toutes ses femmes qui se rejouissoient devant elle de la bonne mine de son serviteur. La seule Victoria demeura froide et serieuse dans les emportemens des autres. Elvire le remarqua et la tira à part pour luy dire qu'elle s'estonnoit de ce qu'elle ne luy disoit rien de l'hereux choix que son pere avoit fait d'un Gendre qui paroissoit avoir tant de merite et ajousta qu'au moins, par flaterie ou par civilite, elle luy devoit dire quelque chose. Madame, luy dit Victoria.... Elvire fut fort estonnée de ce que luy dit sa Gouvernante; elle la pria de ne differer pas davantage à luy exclarcir les doutes qu'elle luy avoit mis dans l'esprit. Victoria luy dit que cela ne se pouvoit dire devant ses servantes, ni en peu de paroles. Elvire feignit d'avoir affaire en sa chambre ou Victoria luy dit.... [73]

Notice how the intrigue is better constructed in the second Spanish version and how Scarron follows it. This second story is also more concerned with punishing impetuosity than with honor. The duel in the first story serves to give Dom Fernand back his honor. This is not present here. A brother that will avenge the family honor is also lacking here. However, there is some mention of honor in this second story which Scarron changes. Compare the following statements:

> Engañado estais, don Pedro, que no soy quien pensays, sino doña Victoria de Silva, a quien debeis su honor, y el me has obligado a ponerme en servicio de la señora doña Brianda, sirviéndola de dueña. [74]

> Et pour vous, adjousta-t-il, vous ne pouvez plus desadvouer que Victoria Portocarrero ne soit votre femme. Victoria se

---

[73] Scarron, *op. cit.*, pp. 652-653.
[74] Castillo Solórzano, *La garduña de Sevilla*, p. 292.

fit alors connoistre a son Infidele qui se trouva le plus confus homme du monde. Elle luy reprocha son ingratitude. [75]

The change in theme is performed by Scarron so as to tie the story to the rest of the novel. The impetuosity of this story serves to point to the kidnapping in the next chapter of the *Roman comique*. Passion will cause unthinking acts. However, these acts will not be successful.

The story also ties in with the tale of Destin. [76] The two brothers, Verville and Saint-Far, represent the obedient and the impetuous. They are both married; one out of love, the other out of necessity. The same situation is mirrored in this story. Dom Diegue, the obedient lover, marries Elvire. Dom Fernand must marry Victoria out of necessity.

There are in a sense three interpolated stories in the first half of the *Roman comique*: "Histoire de l'amante invisible," the story of Destin and "A trompeur, trompeur et demi." Each story presents a different attitude of man toward woman and love. The first and the last are wrong, in Scarron's thinking, while Destin's is the correct one.

It has been pointed out already how Scarron satirizes Dom Carlos for the idealization of his love. He acts through his imagination and not his judgment. In the third tale, Fernand does not act according to his judgment either. He is impetuous and unthinking. He takes what he wants without realizing the consequences. His "love" for Victoria is one of desire. This desire is as false a love as that which is fed by the imagination. Only Destin exercises his judgment and accepts responsibility without idealizing; thus, his name: he can forge his own destiny since he knows what he wants and will accept the consequences. This is not the case with Dom Fernand or Dom Diegue so it is the women who must be strong and show them what they want.

These three differing attitudes are also brought out in the chapter that precedes the story "A trompeur, trompeur et demi." There,

---

[75] Scarron, *op. cit.*, p. 663.

[76] The *récit* of Destin, as the four interpolated stories in the *Roman comique*, is an imitation of a Spanish work. Scarron uses as his model Calderón de la Barca's *Con quien vengo, vengo*.

Inezilla, married and in love with her husband, who represents the judgment of Destin, has two admirers. One is Roquebrune, the poet, who Scarron satirizes throughout the book. He lives in an ideal world and can not cope with reality as symbolized by the horse he can not ride. The other is La Rancune, a misanthropist who can not love but only desires Inezilla.

In addition, Estoile, in love with Destin, has also two admirers. They are Ragotin and Rappiniere. The character of Ragotin has been discussed already in connection with the first story. He represents, as does both Roquebrune and Dom Carlos, a person that denies reality, and sees the world only through the eyes of his imagination. Her other admirer is Rappiniere, who is already married and only desires Estoile. Thus, he disregards the social structure or the reality of the situation in the same manner as Don Diegue and La Rancune.

In conclusion, the first part of the *Roman comique* forms an organic whole when seen from the point of view of the attitudes of men toward women and reality. The building of imaginary castles in Spain can be as harmful to the man of the bourgeoisie as his bitter misanthropy. Both concepts when carried to extreme remove man from the social structure. Since love must be viwed as a social phenomena, the types of love produced by these extremes will be self-destructive. Again, this is in fact what a novel should be about since as Huet states "l'amour doit être le principal sujet du roman." [76]

---

[76] Pierre Daniel Huet, *De l'origine des romans* in *Œuvres* by Marie Madeleine comtesse de La Fayette. (Paris: Garnier Frères, 1864.)

Chapter IV

LE JUGE DE SA PROPRE CAUSE

The second part of Paul Scarron's *Roman comique* did not appear until 1657, six years after the first part. This second part is different from the first in many ways, mainly in that it has more action and it is more elaborate. The first part dealt mostly with the arrival of the players to Mans, the plays they performed, their different inclinations in love, and the adventures of Ragotin.

The second part takes up these love inclinations and turns them to action: there are several kidnappings. Also, the adventures of Ragotin are somewhat different. In the first part, he had gotten into trouble because of his own clumsiness. Now, many of his adventures are the result of tricks that people play on him. We can mention as examples the adventure of the dead body, and the one where they shrink his clothes and tell him he is ill. These adventures are also more elaborate than the ones in the first part.

This change from simplicity to more elaborateness and more action resembles the change that occurs in *Don Quijote de la Mancha*. Maurice Bardon in his *"Don Quichotte" en France au XVIIe et au XVIIIe siècle,* and other critics, have pointed out that Scarron originally intended writing an imitation of *Don Quijote*, but later changed his mind. These critics also point to many resemblances, particularly in the titles of different chapters. Bardon goes on to state that Scarron "poursuit dans le *Roman comique,* cette campagne au profit du bon goût et du bon sens, que le grand Espagnol avoit menée au début de siècle, et que lui-même avoit déjà, dans son œuvre, inaugurée." [1] Bardon even links Scarron's use of interpolated stories to his admiration for Cervantes:

> Le Don Quichotte, enfin, a suggéré à Scarron l'idée de varier son œuvre en y mêlant quelques nouvelles. Et, de fait, il a intercalé dans la trame même de son roman quatre récits assez brefs tirés d'originaux espagnols, et qu'il a accommodés de son mieux au goût français. [2]

If indeed the above is true, then it is possible that in writing a more elaborate second part, Scarron may have been imitating Cervantes, since the second part of *Don Quijote de la Mancha* narrates more elaborate adventures than the first part. Also notice that Ragotin, like Don Quijote, creates his own adventures in the first part, while he is tricked many times in the second part.

This desire for elaborateness may have also been caused by Scarron's exposure to Spanish literature. However, in analyzing the *Roman comique,* critics like Gustave Reynier and Paul Morillot conclude that Scarron owes very little to those Spanish works that had been pointed out as major influences like the *Viage entretenido* of Agustín Rojas, Quevedo's *El buscón* or the *Lazarillo de Tormes.* But, Scarron did imitate many Spanish stories between the publication of the first and second part of the *Roman comique,* and this constant exposure may have caused a change in attitude. This elaborateness will also be reflected in his later plays, according to Lancaster.

These changing characteristics in his writing are also seen in the first two of the three interpolated stories of the second part. The first story is a *récit* made by La Caverne of her past. It is in the same category as the story of Destin in the first part. This *récit* deals wit injustice. The parents of La Caverne were robbed, and then were mistaken for robbers. Later, her father is murdered by a valet, and the mother is pursued by the baron de Sigognac, although she eventually escapes, taking La Caverne with her. This story mirrors the action of the novel, as all the interpolated stories do. At this point in the novel, Angélique has been kidnapped and La Rap-

---

[1] Maurice Bardon, *"Don Quichotte" en France au XVIIe et au XVIIIe siècle* (Paris: Librairie Ancienne Honoré Champion, 1931), p. 96.
[2] *Ibid.,* p. 99.

pinière is paying Destin's valet to kidnap Estoile. Thus, both the action of the novel and the action of the interpolated story deal with violence and injustice.

The next interpolated story is the subject of our chapter: "Le Juge de sa propre cause." It is the ninth story in the first part of Doña María de Zayas y Sotomayor's *Novelas ejemplares y amorosas*. This first part was originally published in Madrid in 1636 with the title of *Honesto y entretenido sarao*. It is interesting to note that Doña María de Zayas y Sotomayor knew and admired Alonso de Castillo Solórzano.

This *nouvelle* differs in many respects from the ones printed in the first part. First, it is taken from a different author. Secondly it is a Moorish story, but more importantly, the French version is more complex than the Spanish story. This is certainly in keeping with the generally more elaborate tone of this second part. Also, in the many changes that Scarron makes, the reader sees in him the expert craftsman, since by now he is used to adapting Spanish stories: between the first and second parts of the *Roman comique* he had published his *Nouvelles tragi-comiques*. It should be noted that two of these were taken from María de Zayas: "La Précaution inutile" and "L'Adultère innocent."

Scarron may have also taken special care in the construction of this story, since d'Ouville had criticized him the previous year in his *Les Nouvelles amoureuses et exemplaires*, where he included his own version of the "Histoire de L'amante invisible," entitling it "La Belle invisible." That collection also contains a version of "Le Juge de sa propre cause." Thus, Scarron and d'Ouville were rivals, and the former wanted to show d'Ouville that a change in the Spanish version is an improvement.

In addition to the influence of *Don Qujiote,* the more romanesque invention of Scarron in his later years, the influence of Spanish literature, and his quarrel with d'Ouville, we can point to one more reason why this story is so elaborate: the great influence and popularity of the Moorish tales in France. Even before the beginning of the seventeenth century, some of these stories entered France. Jorge de Montemayor's *La Diana*, the pastoral novel that had such a great influence on Honoré d'Urfé's *L'Astrée,* contains an interpolated story dealing with the relationship between the Spanish and Moors. Some similarities between this interpolated story and "Le Juge de sa propre cause" exist: Abindarraez and Jarifa are brought up as brother and sister until they find out that he is a moor, one of the few survivors of the famous Abencerraje family, destroyed by the Moorish ruler on false suspicions.

In "Le Juge de sa propre cause" this type of brotherly relationship is also present, since Sophie is brought up with her brother, and with Dom Carlos and Lucie who were also brother and sister. Whey they grow up, Dom Carlos falls in love with Sophie while Lucie loves Sophie's brother. These two die, and Sophie is not allowed to see Dom Carlos. Again there is a resemblance here since it is Jarifa's father who does not allow Abindarraez to see her. The figure of a lone Moorish prince against a very bright tropical moon is also found in both stories, and both Abindarraez and Mulei are surprised by violence.

In *Don Quijote de la Mancha,* Cervantes also includes a Moorish tale. It is the story of the *Cautivo.* There, a man is captured, while in "Le Juge de sa propre cause" it is Sophie. Scarron probably read this story and became interested in the Moorish tale through it, if he had not yet read the "Historia del Abencerraje y la hermosa Jarifa" which had been translated into French many times: by Nicolas Colin in 1578, Gabriel Chappuys in 1582, by Pavillon in 1603, by Bertanet in 1613, by Remy in 1624, by Vitray in 1631, and others. It should be noted also that Cervantes used his own story of the *Cautivo* for one of his plays, *Los baños de Argel.*

Mateo Alemán in *Guzmán Alfarache* also includes an interpolated Moorish tale: it is the story of Ozmin and Daraja. It resembles the "Historia del Abencerraje y la hermosa Jarifa" in many aspects, including the confrontation of one Moor, valiant and in love, with many Christian soldiers, as he is on his way to see Daraja. This novel, with its interpolated story, was very popular in France, and was translated by Chappuys in 1600 and by Chapelain in 1621.

However, it was in 1608 that the most influential translation of a Spanish story dealing with Moors appeared. It was a translation of a work written in 1595 by Ginés Pérez de Hita: *Historia de los vandos de los Zegries y Abencerrages cavalleros moros de Granada, de las civiles guerras que huvo en ella.* The French title was shortened to *Les Guerres civiles de Grenade.* This novel tells the lives of the last Moorish rulers of Spain, and the civil wars that preceded the fall of their last city, Granada, in 1492 to the Catholic

Kings. It deals mainly with the three major families: Abencerrages, Zegries, and Venegas. Scarron in "Le Juge de sa propre cause," will make an allusion to this work as will be pointed out later.

Voiture, having read this work, went to Spain and visited Granada. He even wrote a *nouvelle* where the lovers, Alcidalis and Zelide, were brought up as brother and sister. Also, as in "Le Juge de sa propre cause," she ends up a captive. The reason given in this story is that the countess of Barcelona wants to marry her daughter to Alcidalis, son of the king of Aragon, and thus contrives to banish Zelide, who is loved by Alcidalis.

The same year that Scarron published the second part of the *Roman comique*, Boisrobert published *Les Nouvelles heroïques et amoureuses* containing a story, "L'Heureux desespoir," which is also in this tradition. The influence of these tales continues throughout the century. In 1660 Mlle de Scudéry would publish *Almahide ou l'esclave de la reine,* based on Pérez de Hita's novel. There is a good discussion of its sources in Jerome W. Schweitzer's "George de Scudéry's *Almahide*." [3] In 1670 Mme de La Fayette would publish *Zayde,* while in 1673 Mme de Villedieu would publish the *Galanteries grenadines*. Jean Cazevanne has a discussion of these last two tales and many later ones in "Le Roman Hispano-Mauresque en France."

Discussing Perez de Hita's novel, Cazevanne states:

> Dans cette société que Pérez de Hita nous dépeint guerrière et polie à la fois, sensible, poussant à l'extrême les préceptes de l'honneur et de la galanterie, la femme triomphe. Il semble que, pour tous ces Maures, l'amour soit le seul but de la vie; mais c'est un amour toujours pur, quintessencié. [4]

This element is lacking in the *novela* of María de Zayas. There, the Moors are seen in a bad light; and even the importance of the Moorish prince who gives Sophie her freedom is minimized. Scarron, knowing the vogue of the Moorish tale in France, changes his story

---

[3] Jerome W. Schweitzer, "George de Scudéry's *Almahide,*" *Johns Hopkins Studies in Romance Literature and Languages,* 34 (1939), p. 34.

[4] Jean Cazevanne, "Le Roman Hispano-Mauresque en France," *Revue de la Littérature Comparée,* 5 (1925), p. 597.

to increase this Moorish element, to add a love story dealing with Moors and Christians and tries to establish that spirit of chivalry present in all previous stories mentioned, only lacking in María de Zayas. It is interesting to note that it is this very chivalric element that he condemned through satire in the "Histoire de l'amante invisible" where he alluded to the *Amadis*.

In "Le Juge de sa propre cause" as in the other two interpolated stories taken from the Spanish, Scarron tries to change the Spanish version so as to increase the simplicity and clarity; however, here these changes are less important.

First, Scarron eliminates needless detail. For example, the Spanish story contains a sonnet sung by Claudia at Dom Carlos' request and delicated to Estela.[5] This sonnet is not found in the French version.

Scarron also prefers generalities to particular details, a characteristic of classicism. María de Zayas likes to mention a specific time, while Scarron, as in "A trompeur, trompeur et demi" where he avoided stating the exact time for the lovers' rendezvous, prefers to avoid a specific detail. Here are both passages:

> Las doce serian de la noche cuando Estela y Claudia, cargadas de dos pequeños lios en que llevaban sus vestidos y camisas y otras cosas necessarias à su viage, se salieron de casa.[6]

> Ce jour, que je croyois bien-hereux, arriva. Nous sortimes de la maison, et de la ville.[7]

Notice also that Scarron found it unnecessary to mention that they took their clothes with them. Later on, María de Zayas states the exact title given to Estela by Charles V: "Confirmó á Estela el estado que la dió, añadiéndole el de princesa de Buñol."[8] Scarron sees no reason for such exactness and only states: "et donna à ce

---

[5] María de Zayas y Sotomayor, *Novelas ejemplares y amorosas* (Paris: Baudry, Librería Europea, 1847), p. 159.

[6] *Ibid.*, p. 163.

[7] Paul Scarron, *Le Roman comique* in *Romanciers du XVIIe siècle*, Antoine Adam, ed. (Paris: Bibliothèque de la Pléiade, 1962), p. 741.

[8] Zayas y Sotomayor, *op. cit.*, p. 170.

bienheureux Amant une Principauté dont ses descendans jouissent encore." [9]

There are also mythological allusion in María de Zayas' story that Scarron considers unnecessary, since they only serve as adornments. As stated above, he ridiculed such allusions before, when at the beginning of the *Roman comique,* after a long discussion of the sun's chariot, he finally stated: "Pour parler plus humainement et plus intelligiblement, il estoit entre cinq et six quand une charette entra dans les Halles du Mans." [10]

Consistent in this dislike, Scarron eliminates a very apt allusion found in the Spanish story. When Estela dissappears, leaving a letter stating that don Carlos has kidnapped her, her parents inform him of this telling him that: "él era el autor de este robo, y el Júpiter de esta bella Europa." [11]

Scarron also eliminates many of the sententious sayings found in the Spanish version. The letter, written by Estela to her parents when she leaves the house to elope with don Carlos, mentions the fact that her parents care only about material possessions while she cares about love. María de Zayas makes it into a sententious saying, while Scarron is very informal about it:

> Mal se compadece amor é interes, por ser muy contrario el uno del otro. [12]

> Un merite aussi grand que le sien ne me pouvoit donner que beaucoup d'amour et, quand l'esprit d'une jeune personne en est prevenu, l'interest n'y peut trouver de place. [13]

In the Spanish version, after Estela, disguised as the *Virrey,* tells don Carlos that the reason he woke up so early is that he has a guilty conscience, he responds with a sententious saying which is absent in Scarron:

> Es tan amada la libertad, señor excelentísimo, que cuando no tuviera tan fuertes enemigos como tengo, el alborozo

---

[9] Scarron, *op. cit.,* p. 755.
[10] *Ibid.,* p. 532.
[11] Zayas y Sotomayor, *op. cit.,* p. 162.
[12] *Ibid.,* p. 162.
[13] Scarron, *op. cit.,* p. 747.

> de que me he de ver con ella por mano de vuestra excelencia era bastante á quitarme el sueño; porque de la misma manera que mata un gran pesar lo suele hacer un contento de suerte que el temor del mal y la esperanza del bien hacen un mismo efecto.[14]

María de Zayas y Sotomayor, a believer that *novelas* should be didactic, expresses in a sententious saying the moral of the story at the end. This is not present in Scarron who ends his story with the happiness of marriage. It is also in direct contrast with the end of the "Histoire de l'amante invisible" where Scarron ends his story in a satiric manner. Here is what Zayas states:

> Estela, cuya prudencia y disimulacion la hizo severo juez, siéndolo de su misma causa; que no es menos maravilla que las demas, que haya quien sepa juzgarse á sí mismo en mal ni bien; porque todos juzgamos faltas agenas, y no las nuestras propias.[15]

Even though the Spanish story ends with a didactic statement, it is not necessarily a serious story. This last statement in fact, has very little to do with the *novela* since Estela is not really judging herself, but don Carlos. The French story, as will be discussed later, has probably a more serious purpose, since Scarron understood that the story dealt mainly with justice, and changed it to fit his concept of justice.

María de Zayas has a different style from Alonso de Castillo Solórzano. The speeches made by her characters are always bombastic and filled with successive exclamations. Scarron incorporates some of these in his story. However, he eliminates many of them. When the Moorish king sees Hamete mistreating Estela, he utters several exclamations which are absent from the French text:

> ¿Qué haces, perro? ¿En la corte del rey de Fez se ha de atrever ninguno á forzar las mujeres? Déjala al punto, sino por vida del rey que te mato.[16]

---

[14] Zayas y Sotomayor, *op. cit.*, p. 168.
[15] *Ibid.*, p. 171.
[16] *Ibid.*, p. 164.

Claudia, when she discovers that don Carlos and Estela are going to elope, considers that there is no hope for her. She goes home and cries. If both versions are compared, we can see how the Spanish version is bombastic and rhetorical, while Scarron's version has simplicity and is at the same time more informal:

> Todo esto oyó Claudia, y como le llegasen al alma estas nuevas, recogióse en su aposento, y pensando estar sola, soltando las corrientes á sus ojos, empezó á decir: Ya, desdichada Claudia, ¿qué tienes que esperar? Cárlos y Estela se casan, amor esta de su parte, y tiene pronunciada contra mí cruel sentencia de perderle. ¿Podrán mis ojos ver á mi ingrato en brazos de su esposa? No, por cierto: pues lo mejor será decirle quién soy, y luego quitarme la vida. Estas y otras muchas razones decia Claudia, quejándose de su desdicha; cuando sintió llamar á la puerta de su estancia. [17]

> J'en fus affligée jusqu'a en estre malade et malade jusqu'à en garder le lict. Un jour que je me plaignois à moy-mesme de ma triste destinée et que la croyance de n'estre ouie de personne me faisoit parler aussi haut que si j'eusse parlé à quelque confident de mon amour, je vis paroistre devant moy le Maure Amet. [18]

Notice in Zayas the personification of love, which may be considered a mythological allusion; and also the metaphor used to describe her tears. Both of these adorments are absent from Scarron's version. However, in contrast to the very few changes which improve the clarity and simplicity of the *nouvelle,* there are in this story many other changes that have nothing to do with classical forms or clarity of expression.

As opposed to the interpolated stories already discussed, the French version of "El Juez de su causa" has an almost radical change in the structure. The Spanish story is told in almost chronological order. It begins with the love of don Carlos for Estela in Valencia. Scarron begins his story in Africa, at the very moment when the Moor Hamete is trying to rape Sophie (Estela) and her cries are overheard by the prince of Fez. Thus, Scarron begins his

---

[17] *Ibid.,* p. 160.
[18] Scarron, *op. cit.,* pp. 737-738.

story *in medias res,* at the point of greatest interest. The reader has already seen how he had a similar beginning in "A trompeur, trompeur et demi" where he began the story when Dom Fernand, after being robbed, is brougth in front of Victoria. In that story, however, Scarron had two versions to choose from, and he chose the best. Here he must change the story without having a second text for reference. As stated before, this change links the story to the heroic or adventure movels of the time, since they usually begin at the crisis, and then the *récits* relate what occurred previously. This change in structure shows a Scarron that is now master of the novelesque tradition, and does not need to follow a model. According to G. Hainsworth, this knowledge of the craft of story writing, and particularly this beginning *in medias res* shows the influence of the Spanish *novela* in Scarron:

> C'est à Scarron que nous sommes redevables de ce début pittoresque et frappant. Il faut ajouter cependant, que l'auteur français, en retouchant ainsi la turquerie de María de Zayas, ne fait, au fond, que rendre aux nouvellistes espagnols leur propre bien. Cervantes, dans son *Amante liberal,* Lugo y Dávila, dans son *Premiado el amor constante,* lui enseignaient cet art de présenter d'une manière attrayante une intrigue romanesque. L'on peut même croire qu'au moment de traduire ce récit de María de Zayas, Scarron avait très présent à l'esprit celui de Lugo y Dávila, reproduit en 1628 par Lancelot, et dont le début est très analogue à ce qu'on trouve dans *Le Juge de sa propre cause.* [19]

Scarron's story then continues with Sophie's *récit* of her past life: how she was raised in Valencia along with Dom Carlos, a neighbor, and how they were in love, a sentiment sanctioned by their parents, and how later an Italian count had lured her father with his money. She had then been forbidden to speak with Dom Carlos, and ordered to marry the rich count. It it at this point that the lovers planned to escape.

The place for this *récit* was not entirely Scarron's invention. The Spanish version states that after the Moorish prince saves Estela, she, "después de haberle dicho que era cristiana, con las más breves

---

[19] G. Hainsworth, *Les "Novelas Ejemplares" de Cervantes en France au XVIIe siècle* (Paris: Librairie Ancienne Honoré Champion, 1933), p. 180.

razones que pudo contó su historia." [20] It is approximately here that Scarron places his *récit*.

Sophie is conducted to a ship, guided by Dom Carlos' valet, where she learns that she has fallen into a trap, and is being turned into a slave by Moors. It is at this point that Scarron includes a second *récit* within the first. This adds to the complexity of the story, but serves a purpose. In the Spanish story we find out what will happen, since Zayas states that Dom Carlos' valet is really Claudia, a lady who loves him and who, when she finds out that they are going to elope, makes a deal with a Moor, Hamete, to have Sophie kidnapped and made a slave in Fez.

Scarron does not mention this until Claudia tells her story aboard the Moorish ship. The result is that Sophie is as astonished as the reader. The creation of suspense is an essential preoccupation in Scarron. Again, Scarron was not totally original in his placing of this *récit*, since María de Zayas states that Estela "pidió á Claudia que le dijese qué enigmas eran aquellos que pasaban por ella; la cual se lo contó todo como pasaba." [21]

Thus, Scarron creates his own structure out of María de Zayas' instructions. When Sophie thinks she is eloping with Carlos but finds out that she is actually being kidnapped by the Moors and Claudia, she leaves a letter addressed to her parents in which she stated she was eloping with Dom Carlos. María de Zayas tells the reader about this letter immediately when it happens. She also tells the reader that Dom Carlos was then accused of murdering Sophie but that he escapes from Valencia. In Scarron we do not find out about this letter or about Dom Carlos' escape until he finds Sophie disguised as Dom Fernand, serving the king. He then becomes a good friend of the supposed Dom Fernand and tells him his story. This witholding of detail also adds to the suspense.

The rest of the story is structurally very similar to Zayas': Charles V gives Dom Fernand the viceroyalty of Valencia. Carlos goes there with Dom Fernand, and the latter absolves him of his supposed crime at a trial by revealing that he is actually Sophie. The only change is the fact that in Scarron they spend some time in Paris before going back to Spain.

---

[20] Zayas y Sotomayor, *op. cit.*, p. 165.
[21] *Ibid.*, p. 161.

This radical change in structure through the introduction of *récits* and the *in medias res* beginning may mean that Scarron used another source. However, this is not likely since the *récits* are introduced where María de Zayas stated that there were such *récits*. Also, Scarron prefered the *in medias res* beginning as exemplified in "A trompeur, trompeur et demi."

There are also many similarities in detail that point to the fact that Scarron was not only inspired by the story found in the *Novelas ejemplares y amorosas* of Doña María de Zayas y Sotomayor, but that he had the text in front of him while he wrote his version. When Sophie (Estela) is placed in the Moorish boat, she asks Claudia to explain what is happening. In both versions she uses the word "enigma":

> Pidió a Claudia que le dijese qué enigmas eran aquellos. [22]

> Explique-moy ces Enigmes, luy dis-je. [23]

Also, the historical setting is identical in both tales:

> Sucedió el caso referido, en Fez, a tiempo que el césar Cárlos V, emperador y rey de España, estaba sobre Tunez contra Barbaroja. [24]

> Charles-Quint, en ce temps-la faisoit la guerre en Affrique et avoit assiégé la ville de Tunès. [25]

The night before his trial, Dom Carlos goes to see Dom Fernand, the Visceroy, and again pleade for his innocence. A comparison of both versions shows an almost literal translation:

> La noche ántes entró don Carlos á la misma cámara donde el virey estaba en la cama, y arrodillado ante él, le dijo: Para mañana tiene vuestra excelencia determinado ver mi pleito, y declarar mi innocencia; demas de los testigos que he dado en mi descargo, y han jurado en mi abono, sea el mejor y mas verdadero un juramento que en sus

---

[22] *Ibid.*
[23] Scarron, *op. cit.*, p. 736.
[24] Zayas y Sotomayor, *op. cit.*, p. 165.
[25] Scarron, *op. cit.*, p. 743.

> manos hago, pena de ser tenido por perjuro, de que no solo no llevé á Estela, mas que desde el dia ántes no la ví, ni sé qué se hizo, ni dónde está; porque si bien yo habia de ser su robador, no tuve lugar de serlo con la grande priesa con que mi desdicha me la quitó, ó para mi perdicion ó la suya. Basta, Cárlos, dijo Estela, vete á tu casa, y duerme seguro: soy tu dueño, causa para que no temas; mas seguridad tengo de tí de lo que piensas, y cuando no la tuviera, el haberte traido conmigo y estar en mi casa, fuera razon que te valiera. Tu causa está en mis manos, tu inocencia y la sé, mi amigo eres, no tienes que encargarme mas esto, que yo estoy bien encargado de ello. [26]

> La veille de ce jour fatal, qui tenoit en suspens toute la ville de Valence, Dom Carlos demanda una audience particuliere au Viceroy que la luy accorda. Il se jette à ses pieds et luy dit ces paroles: C'est demain, Monseigneur, que vous devez faire connoistre à tout le monde que je suis innocent. Quoy que les témoins que j'ay fait ouir me dechargent entierement du crime dont on m'accuse, je viens encore jurer à vostre Altesse, comme si j'estois devant Dieu, que non seulement je n'ay pas enlevé Sophie, mais que, le jour devant qu'elle ne fust enlevée, je ne la vis point, je n'eus point de ses nouvelles et n'en ay pas eu depuis. Il est bien vray que je la devois enlever, mais un malheur qui jusqu'ici m'est inconnu la fit disparoistre, ou pour ma perte, ou pour la sienne. C'est assez, Dom Carlos, luy dit le Viceroy, va dormir en repos. Je suis ton Maistre et ton amy, et mieux informé de ton innocence que tu ne penses et, quand j'en pourrois douter, je serois obligé a n'estre pas exact a m'en eclaircir puisque tu es dans ma maison et de ma maison et que tu n'es venu icy avec moy que sous la promesse que je t'ay faite de te proteger. [27]

Again, when Dom Carlos is presenting his case in front of the jury, he states that he loved Sophie, but that he did not kidnap or murder her. Dom Fernand forces him then to say that he still loves Sophie. This is present in both versions. Notice, however, that where the Spanish version uses the definite tense of past action, the preterite, Scarron uses the imperfect, instead of the *passé simple,* thus leaving the statement ambiguous:

---

[26] Zayas y Sotomayor, *op. cit.,* pp. 167-168.
[27] Scarron, *op. cit.,* p. 751.

"LE JUGE DE SA PROPRE CAUSE" 91

> Digo que adoré a Estela. Di que la adoro, replicó el virey algo bajo, que te haces sospechoso en hablar de pretérito, y no sentir de presente. Digo que la adoro, respondió don Cárlos, admirado de lo que en el virey veia. [28]

> Et je luy dis encore que j'aymay, que j'adoray Sophie. Dis que tu l'adores, ingrat! l'interrompit le Viceroy, surprenant tout le monde. Je l'adore, reprit Dom Carlos fort estonné de ce que le Viceroy venoit de dire. [29]

More striking than the simplifications and similarities, or even the changes in structure is the added elaborateness of the French version. In the two previous interpolated stories, Scarron eliminated many of the sententious sayings present in the Spanish versions. Here, however, he keeps some of the sententious sayings found in the Spanish version. When Claudia understands that Hamete has kidnapped not only Sophie, but also herself, she reproaches Hamete. In both versions, he answers with a sententious saying:

> Al traidor, Claudia, respondió Hamete, paragarle en lo mismo que ofende es el mejor acuerdo del mundo, demas que no es razon que ninguno se fie del que no es leal a su misma nacion y patria. [30]

> Je t'ay desja dit que, qui a pû trahir un Maistre, comme toy, meritoit bien d'estre trahie. [31]

Again, when Dom Carlos gets up early the morning of his trial and goes to see the supposed Dom Fernand, he greets Dom Carlos with a sententious saying in both versions, filled with suspicion:

> Madrugado has, amigo Carlos, algo hace sospechosa tu inocencia y tu cuidado, porque el libre duerme seguro de cualquiera pena, y no hay mas cruel acusador que la culpa. [32]

> Et le Viceroy ne le vit pas plustost qu'il luy reprocha qu'il s'estoit levé bien matin pour un homme accusé qui se

---

[28] Zayas y Sotomayor, *op. cit.*, p. 169.
[29] Scarron, *op. cit.*, p. 754.
[30] Zayas y Sotomayor, *op. cit.*, p. 161.
[31] Scarron, *op. cit.*, p. 739.
[32] Zayas y Sotomayor, *op. cit.*, p. 168.

vouloit faire croire innocent, et luy dist qu'une personne qui ne dormoit point se devoit sentir sa conscience chargée.³³

The question may be asked as to why Scarron preserved some of these sententious sayings. In general, it can be stated that Scarron includes sententious saying because the tenor of this story is very different from the previous ones. Here, we have an imitation of the Spanish-Moorish tales so much liked by the French audiences. These tales are more serious and elaborate than a regular *nouvelle*. Also, the fact that he was in competition with d'Ouville may have made him more susceptible to public taste, and elaborateness in prose was what the public desired. As to why these two sententious sayings were preserved, and not the others, the answer is simple: these two deal with the very theme of the *nouvelle*, while the others do not. The first deals with treason and retributive justice. In an imperfect world, when man commits a crime, he must be punished, just as the innocent victim was punished by him. This type of justice is necessary since the order is always being disrupted, and the disruptive element must be curbed.

Justice is the theme not only of this story, but of the second part of the *Roman comique*. The statement of Hamete could have just as well appeared when Saldagne kidnapped Estoile from her first kidnapper, Destin's valet. This similarity should not pass unnoticed since these interpolated stories always mirror the action of the novel: both events deal with a servant who deceived his master and is in turn deceived by someone else.

The second sententious saying which stated that a man who does not have a clear conscience can not sleep, deals with his lack of harmony with his surroundings, and how justice alone can bring order. It may have been said to Rappiniere, when he remained awake thinking his wife was deceiving him, and instead of catching her, caught a goat. He was the guilty party since he desired Estoile, while his wife was faithful.

In addition to preserving some sententious sayings from the Spanish version, Scarron adds some that are not present in María

---

³³ Scarron, *op. cit.*, p. 752.

de Zayas' *novela*. When the Moorish prince is battling with Hamete, and is about to lose the fight, Scarron adds:

> Mais le ciel, qui protege d'ordinaire ceux qu'il éleve au-dessus des autres, fit heureusement passer les gens du Prince assez prés de là pour ouyr le bruit des combattans et les cris des deux femmes. [34]

This statement, in addition to adding to the seriousness of the story, imparts upon the Moorish prince a sense of importance by being in the right and fighting for God's cause. The glorification of the Moors, which is absent from Zayas' story, is very important in Scarron's version. Discussing why Sophie should be dressed as a man when she goes on a ship, Scarron again moralizes:

> La probité ne se rencontre guere sur un vaisseau; la bonne foy n'y est guere mieux gardée qu'à la guerre; et, en quelque lieu que la beauté et l'innocence se trouvent les plus foibles, l'audace des mechans se sert de son avantage et se porte facilement à tout entreprendre. [35]

This statement again points out how justice is retributive, and not prevalent in this world. Thus, to find it, one must work.

To emphasize how Dom Carlos' suffering at the loss of Sophie has made him dejected and suspicious, Scarron, in Dom Carlos' *récit,* states the belief that chance is the master of everything. This sententious saying goes against Sophie's and Scarron's belief. As she will state and the story will prove, justice is finally achieved, even though it may require much suffering. Thus, this sententious saying is present to emphasize how Dom Carlos has strayed from orthodox belief; and even though it emphasizes his love for her, it also emphasizes the fact that he is not the hero:

> Le hazard est maistre de toutes choses et prend souvent plaisir à confondre nos raisonnemens par des succez les moins attendus. [36]

---

[34] *Ibid.*, p. 728.
[35] *Ibid.*, p. 742.
[36] *Ibid.*, p. 746.

Contrary to his practice, Scarron adds not only sententious sayings but also similes. At the very beginning of the story, when the Moorish prince is riding alone along the ocean, Scarron uses a simile. The need for adornment here is because the prince is the central male character in the story, and is depicted as a lonely and romanesque hero of an exotic region. We must remember that Scarron also indulged himself in sententious sayings when he was describing him. This romanesque quality is essential to this type of Moorish story, as evidenced in the "Historia del Abencerrage y la hermosa Jarifa." The following is the simile that Scarron uses:

> Le Prince Maure, galopant le long du rivage, se divertissoit a regarder la Lune et les Estoiles, qui paroissoient sur la surface de la Mer comme dans un miroir. [37]

As in the other stories, Scarron, knowing how the French liked descriptions of the customs of exotic countries, adds such explanations whenever pertinent. In the same manner that he describes assignations at churches in the "Histoire de l'amante invisible," and in the same way that he told the reader of "A trompeur, trompeur et demi" about Spanish *dueñas,* here Scarron tells us why no one in Fez could see the beauty of Sophie:

> Les deux femmes ne furent connues de personne, à cause que les Maures (les plus jaloux de tous les hommes) ont un extreme soin de cacher aux yeux de tout le monde leurs femmes et leurs esclaves. [38]

Discussing the beauty of the night in which the Moorish prince was out riding, Scarron compares it unfavorably with the French night. This adds to the romanesque and exotic quality of the story:

> Le Ciel estoit sans le moindre nuage; la Mer estoit calme et la Lune et les Estoiles la rendoient toute brillante, enfin, il faisoit une de ces belles nuicts des Pais chauds qui sont plus agreables que les plus beaux jours de nos regions froides. [39]

---

[37] *Ibid.,* p. 727.
[38] *Ibid.,* p. 728.
[39] *Ibid.,* p. 727.

"LE JUGE DE SA PROPRE CAUSE" 95

In addition to the many changes in the basic structure already discussed, the French version changes or adds many details for specific purposes. Some of these changes are made, as the changes made in the structure, to add to the suspense of the tale.

Claudia, seeing that Sophie would not surrender to Hamete as she had surrendered to his brother, deceives her by stating that she wants to help her escape, while in reality this was only a trap, since Hamete was waiting in the desert to force her to submit to his will. Scarron witholds the fact that Claudia is lying to Sophie so that when she discovers she has fallen into a trap, her surprise coincides with the reader's surprise. Zayas tells the reader in advance so there is no suspense:

> Desesperado pues del remedio, pidió á Claudia con muchas lástimas diese órden de que por lo menos, usando de la fuerza, pudiese gozarla: prometióselo Claudia; y así un dia que estaban solas, porque las demas eran idas al baño, le dijo la traidora Claudia estas razones.... Arrojóse Estela á los piés de Claudia, y la suplicó que pues era esta su determinacion, que no la dejase, y veria con las veras que la servia. [40]

> Un jour que toutes les autres femmes de la maison estoient allées aux bains publics, comme c'est la coustume de vous autres Mahometans, elle me vint trouver où j'estois, ayant le visage composé à la tristesse, et me parla en ces termes: .... Je me jettay aux pieds de Claudia et, jugeant d'elle par moy-mesme, je ne doutay point de la sincerite de ces paroles. Je la remerciay de toutes les forces de mon expression et de toutes celles de mon ame; je ressentis la grace que je croyais qu'elle me vouloit faire. [41]

Some changes or additions are found in Scarron's version to improve either motivation or verisimilitude. For example, Zaide, Hamete's brother, is on the ship with the two kidnapped Spanish ladies in Scarron, while in María de Zayas, Zaide does not see Claudia until they arrive in Fez. Scarron's version adds to the verisimilitude of the tale because Claudia, although a woman that has performed evil actions, is not necessarily a total villain, and

---

[40] Zayas y Sotomayor, *op. cit.*, p. 163.
[41] Scarron, *op. cit.*, p. 741.

should not surrender to Zaide immediately on arrival at Fez, without having known him previously. Scarron allows for time to pass while they are in the ship, so that Claudia's crime may come after a reasonable time. This procedure was also used by Scarron in "A trompeur, trompeur et demi," where Dom Carlos is given a longer time with Victoria than the character in Castillo Solórzano's story.

In María de Zayas' story, it is stated that after the kidnapping they soon arrived at Fez. Scarron has a longer explanation, since he knew that Fez was not a port, and that the captives had to arrive at a port and then be transported by land to Fez. This again adds to the verisimilitude of the story:

> Y vamos á Estela y Claudia, que en compañía del cruel Hamete navegaban con próspero viento la vuelta de Fez, que como llegasen á ella, fueron llevadas las damas en casa del padre del moro. [42]

> Le bruit que firent en mesme temps les Matelots qui estoient prest d'entrer dans le port de la ville de Salé et l'artilìerie du vaisseau, à laquelle repondit celle du port, interrompirent les reproches que se faisoient Amet et Claudia et me delivrerent pour un temps de la veue de ces deux personnes odieuses. On se debarqua, on nous couvrit les visages d'un voile, à Claudia et à moy, et nous fusmes logées, avec le perfide Amet, chez un Maure de ses parens. Dés le jour suivant on nous fit monter dans un chariot couvert et prendre le chemin de Fez ou, si Amet y fut receu de son pere avec beaucoup de joye, j'y entray la plus affligée et plus desesperee personne du monde. [43]

Notice that in addition to adding details to make the story truer to life, Scarron adds comments on the customs of the country, and also adds many superlatives, which is a trait found very commonly in his writings. María de Zayas does not use so many superlatives, although her style is bombastic.

María de Zayas states that when Sophie left Fez with the help of the Moorish prince, she did so in men's clothes. We are never told why. Scarron adds an explanation which also adds to the verisimilitude of the story:

---

[42] Zayas y Sotomayor, *op. cit.*, p. 162.
[43] Scarron, *op. cit.*, p. 739.

> Le trajet estoit long jusqu'en Espagne, dont les Marchands ne traffiquoient point à Fez. Et, quand elle eust pû trouver un vaisseau Chrestien, belle et jeune comme elle estoit, elle pouvoit trouver entre les hommes de sa Loy ce qu'elle avoit eu peur de trouver entre les Maures. [44]

In the Spanish story, Sophie is allowed to leave Fez by herself. She is given no servant. Scarron adds that she was accompanied by two other Christian captives, one of them a woman in men's dress. This is essential to the verisimilitude of the story since it is necessary for a person of Dom Fernands' fame later on to have a valet to remove his clothes, and this could only be done by another lady. Here are both versions.

> Sabiendo pues Estela esto, mudando su trage mujeril en el de varon, cortándose los cabellos, acompañada solo de su cautivo español, que el príncipe de Fez le mandó dar, juramentándole que no habia de decir quién era.... [45]

> Zoraide conseilla à Sophie de s'habiller en homme puisque sa taille, avantageuse plus que celle des autres femmes, facilitoit ce deguisement. Elle luy dit que c'estoit l'avis de Mulei qui ne trouvoit personne dans Fez à qui il la pust seurement confier; et elle luy dit aussi qu'il avoit eu la bonté de pouvoir à la bienseance de son sexe, luy donnant une compagne de sa croyance et travestie comme elle et qu'elle seroit ainsi garentie de l'inquietude qu'elle pourroit avoir de se voir seule dans un vaisseau entre des soldats et des Matelots. [46]

Again, María de Zayas does not explain how Sophie gets from Fez to Tunez since the Moors and the Christians were at war at this time. Scarron must add these details to increase the verisimilitude of the *novela*:

> Y habiéndose despedido de los dos caballeros moros que la acompañaban, se fué a Tunez, hallándose al servicio del emperador. [47]

---

[44] *Ibid.*, p. 742.
[45] Zayas y Sotomayor, *op. cit.*, p. 165.
[46] Scarron, *op. cit.*, p. 742.
[47] Zayas y Sotomayor, *op. cit.*, p. 165.

> Charles-Quint...avoit envoyé un Ambassadeur à Mulei pour traitter de la rançon de quelques Espagnols de qualité qui avoient fait naufrage à la coste de Maroc. Ce fut à cet Ambassadeur que Mulei recommanda Sophie sous le nom de Dom Fernand, Gentil-homme de qualité, qui ne vouloit pas estre connu par son nom veritable; et Dorotée et son frere passoient pour estre de son train, l'un en qualité de Gentil-homme, et l'autre de Page. [48]

Again, María de Zayas states, in the Spanish version, that when Sophie arrived in Tunez and took passage on a Spanish ship, she became a warrior, acquiring fame. There is no reason given for her sudden desire to become a warrior, since what she really wanted was to return to Valencia in order to marry Dom Carlos. Scarron must add an explanation so as to increase verisimilitude and to present the motivation:

> Il joignait l'armée de l'Empereur qui estoit encore devant Tunez. Nostre Espagnole deguizée luy fut presentée comme un Gentil-homme d'Andalousie qui avoit esté longtemps esclave du Prince de Fez. Elle n'avoit assez de sujet d'aymer sa vie pour craindre de la hazarder à la guerre, et voulant passer pour un Cavalier, elle n'eust pû avec honneur n'aller pas souvent au combat, comme faisoient tant de vaillans hommes dont l'armée de l'Empereur estoit pleine. Elle se mit donc entre les Volontaires, ne perdit pas une occasion de se signaler. [49]

Even then, Scarron finds it difficult to convince the reader that Sophie, dressed up as Dom Fernand, was able to become such an excellent warrior, being a woman, calling her "nostre Amazone," [50] and calling her efforts "difficiles a croire." [51]

To make this episode plausible, Scarron had made a long addition at the beginning of the story. Maria de Zayas, a believer in the superiority of women, as pointed out by Lena E. Sylvania in her work, *Doña María de Zayas y Sotomayor: A Contribution to the Study of her Works,* has no problem believing that a lady can

---

[48] Scarron, *op. cit.,* pp. 743-744.
[49] *Ibid.,* p. 744.
[50] *Ibid.*
[51] *Ibid.*

surpass any man in battle.[52] Scarron must find a plausible motive for this capacity although in the *Roman comique* women are stronger spiritually than men. Thus, the French author adds a long narrative about her upbringing:

> J'eus un frere plus jeune que moy d'une anée; il estoit aymable autant qu'on le pouvoit estre; il m'ayma autant que je l'aymay et nostre amitié mutuelle alla jusqu'au point que, lorsque nous n'estions pas ensemble, on remarquoit sur nos visages une tristesse et une inquietude que les plus agreables divertissements de personnes de nostre âge ne pouvoient dissiper. On n'oza donc plus nous separer; nous apprismes ensemble tout ce qu'on enseigne aux enfans de bonne maison de l'un et de l'autre sexe, et ainsi il arriva qu'au grand étonnement de tout le monde, je n'estois pas moins adroitte que luy dans tous les exercises violens d'un cavalier et qu'il reussisoit également bien dans tout ce que les filles de condition sçavent le mieux faire. Une education si extraordinaire fit souhaitter à un Gentil-homme des amis de mon Pere que ses enfans fussent elevez avec nous. Il en fit la proposition a mes parens, qui y consentirent, et le voisinage des maisons facilita le dessein des uns et des autres. Ce Gentil-homme égaloit mon Pere en biens et ne luy cedoit pas en noblesse. Il n'avoit aussi qu'un fils et qu'une fille à peu pres de l'age de mon frere et de moy, et l'on ne doutoit point dans Valence que les deux maisons ne s'unissent un jour par un double mariage.... Mais l'estat heureux de nos amours innocentes fut troublé par la mort de mon aymable frere: une fiévre violente l'emporta en huit jours et ce fut la le premier de mes malheurs, Lucie en fut si touchée qu'on ne put jamais l'empécher de se rendre Religieuse.[53]

As pointed out before, these very close childhood ties are reminiscent of many famous Moorish tales of the time as the "Historia del Abencerrage y la hermosa Jarifa," or even Voiture's tale. Thus, this addition serves not only to add to the motivation and verisimilitude, but also to the Moorish flavor of the tale.

Other details, not found in the Spanish story, are added by Scarron to increase verisimilitude. Although not mentioned in Zayas,

---

[52] Lena E. Sylvania, *Doña María de Zayas y Sotomayor: A Contribution to the Study of her Works* (New York: Columbia University Press, 1922).
[53] Scarron, *op. cit.*, p. 731.

Dom Carlos changes his name in Scarron after he escapes so as not to be recognized and apprehended:

> Elle en fut inquietée le reste du jour, le fit chercher dans le quartier de ces nouvelles trouppes et on ne le trouva pas parce qu'il avoit changé de nom. [54]

Even though Sophie is dressed in mans' clothes, Scarron believes that he must explain why Dom Carlos, her childhood friend and constant lover, does not recognize her. It must be remembered that Scarron belongs to the realistic school, and can not believe that Astrée could not recognize Céladon whe he came back dressed as Alexis. Here is what the author of the *Roman comique* adds:

> Elle le trouva et n'en fut point reconnue, ayant changé de taille, parce qu'elle avait cru, et de visage, parce que le Soleil d'Afrique avoit changé la couleur du sien. [55]

Scarron is definitely conscious of the difficulties that may present themselves to a lady dressed up as a manly warrior. Even at the end of the story, he is careful to clarify that when Sophie became Viceroy, only her faithful servant, who was Dorothée dressed up as a man, was allowed to dress her in the morning. This is not stated by Zayas:

> A poco rato salió el virey de su cámara á medio vestir; mas cubierto el rostro con un gracioso ceño, con el cual, y con una risa á lo falso, dijo.... [56]

> Il se leva ausi tost que le jour parut et, propre et paré plus qu'a l'ordinaire, se trouva au lever de son Maistre; mais je me trompe, il n'entra dans sa chambre qu'apres qu'il fut habillé, car depuis que Sophie avoit déguisé son sexe, la seule Dorotée, déguisée comme elle, et la confidente de son deguisement, couchoit dans sa chambre et luy rendoit tous les services qui, rendus par un autre, luy eussent pu donner connoissance de ce qu'elle vouloit tenir si cache. [57]

---

[54] *Ibid.*, p. 745.
[55] *Ibid.*
[56] Zayas y Sotomayor, *op. cit.*, p. 168.
[57] Scarron, *op. cit.*, p. 751.

Notice how Scarron is humorous and informal here. Scarron also considers that it is too coincidental that the Viceroy of Valencia would die immediately after Dom Fernand had performed great deeds in the army. He also considers it too much honor for a newly arrived soldier such as Dom Fernand to get such a post. Thus, he follows history and the exploits of Charles V until enough time has elapsed so as to make the death of the Viceroy a probable event. He also brings in Paris to make the tale appear even more probable, and realistic although occuring mainly in a remote environment:

> Le Grand Roy qui regnoit alors voulut surpasser en generosité en franchise un mortel ennemy qui l'avoyt tousjours surmonté en bonne fortune et n'en avoit pas tousjours bien usé. Charles-Quint fut receu dans Paris comme s'il eust esté le Roy de France. Le beau Dom Fernand fut du petit nombre des personnes de qualité qui l'accompagnerent et, si son maistre eust fait un plus long sejour dans la Cour du monde la plus galante, cette belle Espagnolle, pris pour un homme, eut donné de l'amour a beaucoup de Dames Françoises et de la jalousie aux plus accomplis de nos Courtisans. [58]

This careful craftsmanship on the part of the French author was probably a result of his quarrel with d'Ouville, and his desire to outshine him in this story, by improving on the Spanish version.

Let us now turn to those changes that alter completely the Spanish story, and that make "Le Juge de sa propre cause" an original *nouvelle*. First of all, Scarron realizes that he is writing a Moorish tale in the tradition of Villegas, Aleman, Montemayor, Perez de Hita, Voiture and others. The Spanish version has very little about Morocco, and what it has, is not sympathetic and much less idealized. The chivalric quality of the Moors present in Pérez de Hita is not found in Zayas. Scarron adds several Moorish characters to contrast their nobleness to the villany of Hamete and his brother Zayde. Those that are added are Zulema and his wife Zeraide who "avoit la reputation d'estre la plus belle femme de Fez et aussi spirituelle que belle." [59]

---

[58] *Ibid.*, p. 750.
[59] *Ibid.*, p. 729.

They are the ones who take care of Sophie after the Moorish prince rescues her from Hamete. Scarron may have taken the name of Zeraide from the story of the *Cautivo* by Cervantes, where she is the heroine. When the time for Sophie's departure arrives, the Moorish couple can hardly part with Sophie:

> Sophie et Zeraide ne se purent quitter sans regret et il y eut bien des larmes versées de part et d'autre. Zeraide donna à la belle Chrestienne un rang de perles si riche qu'elle ne l'eust point receu si cette aymable Maure et son Mary Zulema, qui n'aymoit pas moins Sophie que faisoit sa femme, ne luy eussent fait connoistre qu'elle ne pouvoit davantage les desobliger qu'en refusant ce gage de leur amitié. Zeraide fit promettre a Sophie de luy faire sçavoir de temps en temps de ses nouvelles.[60]

Many of the other changes that take place so as to add a Moorish flavor to the story, deal with the prince, and will be discussed when his role is analyzed. It should be mentioned that there is one detail added by Scarron, that, although increasing the exoticism of the *nouvelle,* does not add to its Moorish qualities. According to Scarron, when Dom Carlos escaped justice at Valencia, and before becoming a soldier for Charles V, he became a bandit. The association of Spain with impossible passion and bandits will survive into the nineteenth century when Mérimée will write his *Carmen* and Théophile Gautier will relate his adventures with bandits in Spain in his *Voyage en Espagne.* Here is what Scarron states:

> Je me joignis à des Bandoulliers, prisonniers comme moy, et tous gens de resolution; nous forçâmes les portes de nostre prison et, favorisez de nos amys, nous eusmes plus tost gagné les Montagnes les plus proches de Valence que le Viceroy n'en peust estre adverty. Nous fusmes longtemps maistres de la Campagne. L'infidelité de Sophie, la persecution de ses parens, tout ce que je croiois que le Viceroy avoit fait d'injustice contre moy et enfin la perte de mon bien, me mirent dans un tel desespoir que je hasarday ma vie dans toutes les rencontres où mes Camarades et moy trouvâmes de la resistance; et je m'acquis par là une telle reputation parmi eux qu'ils voulurent que je fusse leur

---

[60] *Ibid.,* p. 744.

"LE JUGE DE SA PROPRE CAUSE"   103

Chef. Je le fus avec tant de succés que nostre trouppe devint redoutable aux Royaumes d'Aragon et de Valence et que nous eusmes l'insolence de mettre ces pays à contribution.[61]

The theme of the *nouvelle*, as stated before, is justice. Through no fault of their own, Dom Carlos and Sophie find themselves unjustly treated. Sophie comes to know (thus her name) that she must fight her bad fortune in order to be given justice. In other words, she realizes that justice is not prevalent but that it can be gained through effort. Dom Carlos, on the other hand, fights injustice with injustice: he becomes a thief and he even suspects Sophie. He then will not be the hero of the story. The Moorish prince is the hero from the very beginning. Scarron tells us that God does not forget those he favors. Thus, Muley, when he seems lost in his battle with Hamete, finds help from his soldiers. The same is true with Sophie. All alone in the desert with Hamete, she seems lost but is miraculously saved.

In other words, what Scarron is telling us is that justice will exist if we look for it. Destin goes through the *Roman comique* searching for justice. Estoile is unjustly taken from him. But Garouffière arrives and confers justice. He is the one who tells this story. Dom Carlos, on the other hand, is not at all like Destin or Muley. When his dreams are apparently broken, he goes to pieces and believes that chance is the only mistress of the universe. He thus resembles the Dom Carlos of the "Histoire de l'amante invisible" who is not capable of forging hsi own destiny. Like Porcia, and Victoria, Sophie must take matters into her own hands and fight for that justice she thinks belongs to her.

To get his point across, Scarron must make the heroine into a strong woman, as he did in the other two interpolated stories. First of all, our heroine must be beautiful and determined. When the Moorish prince sees her, María de Zayas states that he asks her who she is out of compassion. A totally diferent account is given by Scarron:

> No agradado de su hermosura, sino compasivo de sus trabajos, le pregunto quién era.[62]

---

[61] *Ibid.*, p. 748.
[62] Zayas y Sotomayor, *op. cit.*, p. 165.

> La femme que le Prince avoit secourue le surprit, et toute sa cour aussi, par sa beauté, plus grande que quelque autre qui fust en Affrique et par un air majestueux que ne put cacher aux yeux de ceux qui l'admirerent un mechant habit d'Esclave. [63]

Sophie must also have the courage to brave the world and her fortune. Scarron describes how when Sophie discovers she is being kidnapped, she takes out a dagger and fights Hamete. This is not present in the Spanish version:

> Je me jettay sur luy, nonobstant la foiblesse que m'avoit laissée ma pâmoison et, avec une adresse vigoreuse à quoy il ne s'atendoit pas et que j'avois acquise par mon education, comme je vous ay desja dit, je luy tiray le Cimeterre du fourreau, et je m'allois venger de sa perfidie si son frere Zaide ne m'eust saisi le bras assez a temps pour luy sauver la vie. On me desarma facilement, car ayant manque mon coup, je ne fis point de vains efforts contre un si grand nombre d'ennemis. [64]

When Sophie is taken into the ship where she is to be taken to Fez, she faints in both versions. However, the reason given for her fainting it different:

> Tanto sintió Estela su desdicha, que asi como se vió rodeada de moros, y entre ellos el esclavo de don Cárlos, y que él no parecia, vió que á toda prisa se hacian á la vela, y considerando su desdicha, aunque ignoraba la causa, se dejó vencer de un mortal desmayo que le duró hasta otro dia. [65]

> Ces paroles dites à une femme que je croiois un homme et dans lesquelles je ne pouvois rien comprendre, me causerent un si furieux deplaisir que je tombay comme morte entre les bras du perfide Maure qui ne m'avoit point quittée. [66]

---

[63] Scarron, *op. cit.*, p. 729.
[64] *Ibid.*, p. 735.
[65] Zayas y Sotomayor, *op. cit.*, p. 161.
[66] Scarron, *op. cit.*, p. 734.

The battle between Sophie and Hamete is described differently in both versions. In the French story, Sophie is more courageous than in Zayas' story:

> Y viendo que nada bastaba, quiso usar de la fuerza, batallando con ella hasta rendirla. El ánimo de Estela en esta ocasion era mayor que de una flaca doncella se podia pensar; mas como á brazo partido anduviese luchando con ella, rendidas ya las débiles fuerzas de Estela, se dejó caer en el suelo: y no teniendo facultad para defenderse, acudió al último remedio, y al mas ordinario y comun de las mujeres, que fué dar gritos.[67]

> Ayant plus de vigueur et d'adresse que les femmes n'en ont d'ordinaire, je resistay longtemps aux efforts de ces deux méchantes personnes, mais à la longue, je me sentis affoiblir, et, me défiant de mes forces, je n'avois presque plus recours qu'à mes cris, qui pouvoient attirer quelque passant en ce lieu solitaire.[68]

However, it is necessary not only to be valiant, beautiful, and majestic to be a heroine. One must also have great feelings. Sophie's grief in losing Dom Carlos is poignantly portrayed in Scarron, while Zayas hardly mentions it. When Sophie is at Zeraide's house, she refuses to be consoled:

> Si cette belle Chrestienne eust esté capable de consolation, elle en eust trouvé dans les caresses de Zeraide, mais comme si elle eust evité tout ce qui pouvoit soulager sa douleur, elle ne se plaisoit qu'a estre seule pour pouvoir s'affliger davantage et, quand elle estoit avec Zeraide, elle se faisoit une extreme violence pour retenir devant elle ses soupirs et ses larmes.[69]

The only fault the reader may have found in Sophie is her love for Dom Carlos, who does not seem as worthy of her as Muley. Scarron does admit that this choice may have been made through the imagination, and not realistically. However, there is never any hint that Sophie has ceased to love Dom Carlos:

---

[67] Zayas y Sotomayor, *op. cit.*, p. 164.
[68] Scarron, *op. cit.*, p. 741.
[69] *Ibid.*, pp. 729-730.

> Quand je fus seule, Dom Carlos se representa à mon souvenir comme le plus aymable homme du monde. Je fis reflexion sur tout ce que le Comte Italien avoit de desagreable; je conceus une furieuse aversion pour luy et je sentis que j'aymois Dom Carlos plus que je n'eusse jamais crû l'aymer et qu'il m'estoit également impossible de vivre sans luy et d'estre hereuse avec son Rival.[70]

Just as the heroine's name has been changed from Estela to Sophie to point out that she is the strong character, since she knows what she wants, so the name of the prince has been changed. In the Spanish version he is called Jacimin. Scarron changes his name to Muley. Several rulers of Morocco had this name which is even mentioned by Cervantes in the story of the *Cautivo*. However, there is a character of the same name in Calderon de la Barca's *Principe constante*. In that play, don Fernando captures Muley, a Moorish general from Fez, but lets him go, since he is in love. In Scarron, Muley captures a lady and allows her to go under the name of Dom Fernand because she is in love. Thus, this change in name links Muley to all the chivalric Moorish princes who believe in love as a supreme ideal. In fact, Muley falls in love with Sophie in Scarron's story:

> Il l'avoit fait connoistre a Zulema et, comme il ne luy cachoit rien, il luy avoit aussi avoué qu'il se sentoit porte a aimer la belle Chrestienne et qu'il le luy auroit desja fait sçavoir si la grande affliction qu'elle faisoit paroistre ne luy eût fait craindre d'avoir un rival inconnu en Espagne, qui, tout éloigné qu'il eut esté, l'eust pu empescher d'estre hereux, mesme en un pays où il estoit absolu.[71]

When the prince finds out that Sophie loves another, he believes in her virtue and will not see her even though he will grant her her freedom:

> Encore que tout ce qu'on luy conta de la fortune de la belle Chrestienne ne flattast point la passion qu'il avoit pour elle, il fut pourtant bien aise, virtueux comme il estoit, d'en avoir eu connoissance et d'apprendre qu'elle estoit en-

---

[70] *Ibid.*, p. 732.
[71] *Ibid.*, p. 730.

> gagée d'affection en son païs afin de n'avoir point a tenter une action blâmable par l'esperance d'y trouver de la facilité. Il estima la vertu de Sophie et fut porté par la sienne à tâcher de la rendre moins malheureuse qu'elle n'estoit. Il luy fit dire par Zeraide qu'il la renvoyerait en Espagne quand elle le voudroit.[72]

Muley is then a *parfait amant,* as much in love as Abindarraez, or the Cid, and just as conscious of his duty. He is a lonely and romanesque figure riding in the African desert. He is an absolute ruler and yet his justice is so strict that he will not keep Sophie. This justice is not emphasized in the Spanish version, since there, his father is ruler, and he can not do justice alone:

> Jacimin enojado mandó que á todos tres les trajesen á su palacio, donde ántes de curarse dió cuenta al rey su padre del suceso, pidiéndole venganza del atrevimiento de Hamete.[73]

> Ce jeune Prince commandoit dans Fez aussi absolument que s'il en eust desja este Roy.[74]

The generosity of the prince is also emphasized by Scarron since it goes hand in hand with his justice. While in Zayas, Estela has to plead for her freedom, in Scarron his generosity is spontaneous. Here is the Spanish version:

> A lo cual la dama, arrodillada ante él, le suplicó que la enviase entre cristianos, para que pudiese volver á su patria.[75]

Finally, the story of the captive Christians is told so that the reader will understand how Muley came to know what justice was through experience. This event convinced him that happiness is not achieved through selfishness but by a generous justice, and he is thus able to gran this to Sophie:

---

[72] *Ibid.,* p. 742.
[73] Zayas y Sotomayor, *op. cit.,* p. 165.
[74] Scarron, *op. cit.,* p. 728.
[75] Zayas y Sotomayor, *op. cit.,* p. 165.

> Ce Prince Maure avoit acheté d'un Corsaire une prise qu'il avoit faite sur mer: c'estoit d'un vaisseau du Gouverneur d'Oran qui portoit la famille entiere d'un Gentilhomme Espagnol, que, par animosité, ce Gouverneur envoyoit prisonnier en Espagne. Mulei avoit sçeu que ce Chrestien estoit un des plus grands chasseurs du monde et, comme la chasse estoit la plus forte passion de ce jeune Prince, il avoit voulu l'avoir pour Esclave; et, afin de la mieux conserver, ne l'avoit point voulu separer de sa femme, de son fils et de sa fille. En deux ans qu'il vescut dans Fez au service de Mulei, il apprit a ce Prince à tirer parfaitement l'arquebuze sur toute sorte de gibbier qui court sur la terre ou qui s'eleve dans l'air et plusieurs chasses inconnues aux Maures. Il avoit par la si bien merite les bonnes graces du Prince et s'estoit rendu si necessaire a son divertissement qu'il n'avoit jamais voulu consentir a sa rançon, et par toutes sortes de bienfaits avoit tache de luy faire oublier l'Espagne, mais le regret de n'estre pas en sa Patrie et de n'avoir plus d'esperance d'y retourner luy avoit cause une melancolie qui finit bien-tôst par sa mort et sa femme n'avoit pas vescu longtemps apres son Mary. Mulei se sentoit du remors de n'avoir pas remis en liberte, quand ils la luy avoient demandée, des personnes qui l'avoient meritée par leurs services, et il voulut autant qu'il le pouvoit reparer envers leurs enfans le tort qu'il croyoit leur avoir fait. [76]

This emphasis on justice also brings about other changes in the story. If the letters written by Sophie in each version are compared, it can be seen that Scarron emphasizes injustice, while María de Zayas deals with material gain as the cause of the catastrophe:

> Mal se compadece amor é interes por ser muy contrario el uno del otro, y por esta causa, amados padres mios, al paso que me alejo del uno, me entrego al otro: la poca estimacion que hago de las riquezas del conde me lleva à pedir de don Cárlos, á quien solo reconozco por legítimo esposo: su nobleza es tan conocida que á no haberse puesto de por medio tan fuerte competidor, no se pudiera para darme estado pedir mas ni desear mas. Si el yerro de haberle hecho de este modo merieciere perdon, juntos volveremos á pedirle. [77]

---

[76] Scarron, *op. cit.*, p. 743.
[77] Zayas y Sotomayor, *op. cit.*, p. 162.

> Vous n'avez pas deu me deffendre d'aymer Dom Carlos apres me l'avoir ordonné. Un merite aussi grand que le sien ne me pouvoit donner que beaucoup d'amour et, quand l'esprit d'une jeune personne en est prevenu, l'interest n'y peut trouver de place. Je m'enfuy donc avec celuy que vous avez trouve bon que j'aymasse des ma jeunesse et sans qui il me seroit autant impossible de vivre que de ne mourir pas mille fois le jour avec un estranger que je ne pourrois aymer, quand il seroit encore plus riche qu'il n'est pas. Nostre faute, si c'en est une, merite vostre pardon. Si vous nous l'accordez, nous reviendrons le recevoir plus vite que nous s'avons fuy l'injuste violence que vous nous vouliez faire. [78]

Finally, it should be noted that there is an allusion to the Zegris family.[79] It is mentioned that Zeraide and Zulema are members of that family. Scarron's readers, most probably acquainted with Pérez de Hita's work and with the "Historia del Abencerrage y la hermosa Jarifa," must have wondered why Scarron did not make them instead members of the Abencerrage family, since it was the Zegris' calumnies that brought about the king's injustice and the almost complete extinction of the Abencerrages living in Granada. Just as Muley had to err once before coming to know justice, so Zeraide and Zulema had to know injustice before being able to act with generosity toward the captive, since remorse brings about a realization of justice.

This fact serves to foreshadow Dom Carlos' future. Sophie shows him his injustice toward her, and toward society. His realization of this will teach him the meaning of justice and will help him be a just Viceroy. To conclude, Scarron's version of "Le juge de sa propre cause" forms an integral part of the *Roman comique* by imitating its elaborate tone and by its emphasis on justice. It is very fitting that it be told by Garouffière, the nemesis of the novel.

---

[78] Scarron, *op. cit.*, p. 747.
[79] *Ibid.*, p. 729.

CHAPTER V

LES DEUX FRÈRES RIVAUX

The last interpolated story in the *Roman comique* is "Les deux frères rivaux." The original Spanish tale is not found in María de Zayas' *Novelas amorosas y ejemplares*. Instead, Scarron goes back to Alonso de Castillo Solórzano and takes the story from the same collection that he used for the tales in the first part of the *Roman comique*: *Los alivios de Casandra*. In fact, this is the first story of that collection. The Spanish title is "La confusión de una noche."

Of all the four interpolated stories in the *Roman comique*, this is the one which comes the closest to a literal translation, and thus reminds us of "Los efectos que hace amor," and not of the other story in the second part, "El juez de su causa." It is possible then that Scarron translated this story at the time he translated the first one, since it comes first in *Los alivios de Casandra* and it shows very little sophistication of technique. However, the story does fit in this second part since it has an elaborate plot that matches the elaborate events of the second part. It also has an elaborate style since Scarron left or added some figures of speech. The structure, however, is very simple. The action as will be seen later, mirrors the developments in the novel, as did the other stories.

In "Les deux frères rivaux," Scarron, as in the other stories, creates a greater simplicity and straightforwardness, eliminating many details and adornments of style, although, as stated before, he keeps some and adds others. For example, when Dom Sancho (don Fadrique) goes to the Marquis Fabios' house after he is thought to have died when he leaped from the Turkish ship, he wants to find his old valet in order to send him to Sevilla to get information on the behavious of Dorotée. The French version has a short paragraph stating that the valet was taken out of a monastery where he had gone, grieved over his master's death. The Spanish tale states that he was considering entering a monastery. In addition to this change, the Spanish version is very elaborate on this detail that has little to do with the plot, while the French narrative is short and to the point. For Scarron, the mention of an actual fact, that the valet had gone to a monastery, was sufficient to prove his loyalty, so that the other events are superfluous and do not need relation. Here are both versions:

> Tenia don Fradrique un criado que se avia criado desde niño en casa de sus padres, y les avia servido desde su niñez, este se llamava Leoncio, el qual vino a Napoles con el General donde estava desde que se divulgó la muerte de de don Fadrique, deseava su amo tenerla consigo, y assi pido al marques su huesped, que le escriviesse una carta en que le llamasse que se viniesse con el a Catania, hizolo assi, y esta se la llevó un criado del Marques muy privado suyo, llevando orden del, que Leoncio no quisiesse venirse, le dijese como su dueño vivia, en breves dias se puso Octavio en Napoles donde encontrando con la posada de Leoncio, le halló en ella; diole la carta del Marques, y aunque en ella le instava que viniesse a su casa, huvo de declararle su intencion Leoncio para escusarse justamente con el Marques la qual era entrarse Religioso Descalço: esto avia causado la muerte de don Fadrique su señor a quien amava lealissimamente con la qual desengañado de quan poco durables son los gustos desta vida, se queria acoger a la que esperava seria el eficaz medio de su salvacion; viole Octavio tan puesto en esta determinacion que huvo de valerse del ultimo remedio, diziendole como don Fadrique vivia, y estava bueno y contento en compañia del Marques su dueño, no lo creia Leoncio, antes juzgaba que aquella ficion la avia inventado el desseo de llevarle a Octavio, mas como el le assegurasse la verdad, determinose Leoncio a hazer aquella jornada, que perdia poco en llegarse a Sicilia, pues quado no hallasse por verdad lo que assegurava, le quedava tiempo para poner en execucion su devoto intento, pidio licencia al General, en cuya casa estava, y en breve tiempo se hallaron los dos en Sicilia, y en Catania, donde entrando sin ser visto en casa del Marques halló verdadera la relacion que Octavio le avia

> hecho, con verse en la presencia de don Fadrique, con cuya vista estava loco de contento, diziendo mil disparates de gozo en ver vivo a quien tanto estimava.[1]

> Sanchez, vallet de Dom Sanche, avoit esté si affligé de la perte de son Maistre que, quand les Galeres de Naples vinrent se rafraischir à Messine, il entra dans un Convent pour y passer le reste de ses jours. Le Marquis Fabio l'envoya demander au Superieur, qui l'avoit receu à la recommandation de ce Seigneur Sicilien et qui ne luy avoit pas encore donné l'habit de Religieux. Sanchez pensa mourir de joye quand il revit son cher maistre et ne songea plus a retourner dans son Convent.[2]

Notice that Scarron eliminates the mention of Catania and restricts himself to the mention of Messina in Sicily so as to avoid confusion. The change made by Scarron of having Sanchez already in a monastery should be discussed. The fact that Dom Sanche's valet had already entered into a monastery, thus showing his faithfulness, is present to mirror and contrast with Dorotée's behavior. She must merit Dom Sanche's love by being faithful to him after his death. If a valet can show this kind of loyalty to his master, why not the lady? This image can be compared to the relationship of the knight, the squire, and the lady in a romance of chivalry. However, there is a distinct difference. In those novels, it is the knight that must merit the lady by his deeds of valor. She is only a passive and idealized figure.

The squire, on the other hand, must merit his master's affection through loyalty. In "Les deux frères rivaux," Dom Sanche puts his lady to the test, as well as his valet. She is no longer the passive idealized figure of the romances of chivalry that greatly influenced the heroic novel of the seventeenth century. However, Dom Sanche himself is also put to the test since he is separated from her, and only through courage and endurance can he return to her. Thus, here we have a completely differing concept of love from the romances of chivalry. There, a man must fight for an idealized and

---

[1] Alonso de Castillo Solórzano, *Los alivios de Casandra* (Barcelona: Emprenta de Jayme Romeu, 1640), pp. 23-24.
[2] Paul Scarron, *Le Roman comique* in *Romanciers du XVIIe siècle*, Antoine Adam, ed. (Paris: Bibliothèque de la Pléiade, 1962), p. 785.

distant beauty, and must even do penance as Amadís de Gaula, Don Quijote, Lancelot and Roland. There, a woman is such an ethereal concept that little remains of her actual self. This is in fact the concept of love presented by Scarron in the "Histoire de l'amante invisible." There, Dom Carlos must merit the love of Princess Porcia through his actions. She is a passive figure, and he idealizes her, since he loves her without ever having seen her. Scarron ridiculed this type of love. In "Les deux frères rivaux," love is an interaction between two people. Each must merit the other and neither is idealized. Here also, everything is in its proper perspective, since the woman does not need to be stronger than the man and maneuver to have him marry her. Like Destin, Dom Sanche knows what he wants, and these wants are real. Thus, this story does not contain satire, but is told in a straightforward manner. The conclusion of the story, which will be discussed later, points to the need for this type of love.

Let us return for a moment to the discussion of the valet's action. It indeed mirrors the actions of Dorotée. She did not enter a convent, but, she decided, and told her sister, that she would enter a convent only if her father forced her to marry a man she did not love, and that she only loved Dom Sanche. Thus, she does not enter a convent because she is not forced into anything by her father.

This is in direct contrast to the previous story, "Le Juge de sa propre cause," where Sophie's father tries to force her into a marriage she knows will not succeed. This story blends for Scarron not only the true concept of love, but also a sense of justice since the head of the family, the dispenser of justice, knows how to achieve harmony. It is fitting that "Les deux frères rivaux" be the last story told here, since it mirrors the new harmony achieved in the *Roman comique* after justice has been dispensed and love is placed in its proper perspective. Thus, "Les deux frères rivaux" is a summing up of the themes present in the *Roman comique,* and a glorification of harmony.

Scarron found the story so well suited for his purpose that he made very few changes, although, as stated before, he did try to increase its clarity and simplicity. To achieve straightforwardness, Scarron eliminates many needless details. For example, as background, we are told that Dom Sanche has been fighting in Flanders.

This is stated in passing by Scarron to give an explanation for his abilities:

> Plusieurs Cavaliers de Seville, qui l'avoient connu en Flandres ou il avoit commandé un Regiment de Cavalerie, le convierent de courir la bague avec eux; ce qu'il fit habillé a la soldate.[3]

Castillo Solórzano, on the other hand, gives a long narration of his actions in Flanders that Scarron considers unnecessary:

> Este no contento con militar en aquellos tercios de Napoles, quiso exponer su persona a mayores peligros partiendose a Flandes, donde mostró su valor, siguiendo las banderas de Rey de España, contra los rebelados Olandeses. Allí mereció una bandera, que en pocos dias la trocó en gineta, y dentro de un año governó como Coronel quatro compañias de Coraças, en este cargo se señaló con mas esfuerço que en los demas, pues hallandose en muchas escaramuças contra el enemigo, alcançó del vitoriosos despojos, y eterno nombre en lenguas de la fama, con que le honró el pecho la roja insignia del Patron de las Españas.[4]

When they play these wargames mounted on horses, Castillo Solórzano discusses the horses. Scarron does not mention them because he considers this irrelevant:

> Una tarde que huvo carrera publica en su calle (cosa muy usada otras vezes, y mas con la ocasion de tener esta Ciudad vezindad con la de Cordova, donde las Riberas del claro Bethis cria tan hermosos cavallos que por excelencia los llaman hijos del Viento).[5]

In the Spanish version, Dorotée falls in love with Dom Sanche when she sees him riding his horse in front of her house. She thinks of him all night, and in a few days, she goes to the church where she has occasion to meet him. Scarron only states that Dom Sanche rode his horse one day. No mention is made of Dorotée's seeing

---

[3] *Ibid.*, p. 773.
[4] Castillo Solórzano, *op. cit.*, p. 9.
[5] *Ibid.*

him, and it is the next day in church when she first sees him. Here is a long passage in Castillo Solórzano not present in the French version:

> Todo esto vio la hermosissima Dorotea, y lo que sus pretendientes, desseandola no merecieron en tanto tiempo que la avia festejado, pudo merecer en solas dos horas el forastero Toledano sin desearla, porque aun no avia reparado cuydadosamente en ella, acabóse la fiesta dexando a todos don Fadrique muy pagados de su persona, dandole muchas alabanças por lo diestramente que avia andado en las dos sillas.
> Quedarō Dorotea y Feliciana solas en su quarto quando lo estava la tierra de la luz de Febo y todo el tiēpo q̄ huvo desde cerrar la noche hasta que fueron llamadas a cenar se ocuparon en celebarar las dos la gala de don Fadrique, el despejo con que avia corrido, su buen talle (que le gozava extramado) y finalmente ninguna de sus acciones se quedo sin alabanças, apassionādose en esto mas Dorotea, desseando saber quiē era el forastero, bien conocio su hermana la inclinacion de Dorotea, no poco admirado de ver que la que avia sido tā obligada cō finezas, tan requestada cō papeles, y en fin tan festejada de sus galanes en el primero dia que avia visto a un forastero se le avia inclinado, disculpavala por conocer las partes del, que merecian qualquier favor. Llegósela hora de dar sossiego a los cuerpos cō la porcion del sueño y pudose dar muy poca la hermosa Dorotea, passando toda la noche en desuelo con imaginaciones todas puestas en su nuevo galan, desta suerte continuó algunas noches, quitadose el comer, con que andava con notable melancolia.[6]

The reason for this deletion, in addition to the fact that it is an unnecessary account, is that Scarron was trying to present the way love should be. In Castillo Solórzano we gather that it is through Dorotée's effort that they meet. She then becomes the dominant person of the relationship. Also, that love could become so strong through just a glimpse of him, points to the fact that it is not grounded on reality: notice the use of terms like "inclinación," and "melancolía." In effect, Castillo Solórzano clearly indicates that Dorotée spent the night thinking of fiction and not reality: "con

---

[6] *Ibid.*, p. 10.

imaginaciones." Scarron corrects this by eliminating the paragraph, thus making Dom Sanche the dominant person in the relationship and establishing a different motive other than just *inclinación* for their love. Scarron must have been thinking of Mlle de Scudéry's warning about the *tendre sur inclination* when he deleted this paragraph. The French author is trying to impose harmony and not lead the couple into a "mer dangereuse."

Castillo Solórzano is also careful in his description of dress. Scarron dismisses it as a needless detail. When Dom Sanche enters the church, the Spanish version carefully describes his attire. This is missing in Scarron:

> Porque entrado en la Iglesia con una tropa de cavalleros bizarramete vestidos, entre ellos venia el objeto de nuestra daoma, ya vestido de negro, pero con un vestido de capricho porque era bordado, de noguerado y plata acuchillado todo el en escaramuça sobre lama noguerade, los cabos eran vistosos, conformes a los forros, el jubon riquissimamente bordado con taheli y guantes conformes a el, plumas nogueradas y blancas, y adereço de espada dorado, todo tan luzido que llevava la atencion de todos, alabando su ben talle, aqui se puso habito pendiēte de una rica cadena de diamantes en una venera, los quales eran de gran fondo y mucho precio. [7]

When Dom Diègue, warned by envious ladies, is told that Dorotée has a secret suitor, he disguises himself and spies on them. This disguise is mentioned in passing by Scarron: "Dom Diègue, habillé en pauvre, se posta auprès de la porte du logis." [8] Castillo Solórzano, on the other hand, has to explain where the disguise came from, a needless detail according to Scarron: "Y assi con el vestido de un pobre (que para este efecto desnudo) arrojado en un encoge que avia en la calle por donde don Fadrique entrava a verse con su dama..." [9]

Dom Diègue, a few days later, comes back with help to murder Dom Sanche as he goes to keep his rendezvous. Dom Sanche, however, is carrying two pistols and shoots Dom Diègue while his

---

[7] *Ibid.*, p. 11.
[8] Scarron, *op. cit.*, p. 782.
[9] Castillo Solórzano, *op. cit.*, p. 19.

companions run away. Castillo Solórzano gives us a careful description of the event and what happens to Dom Diègue: Scarron considers this needless detail, and only tells us that Dom Diègue was seriously wounded. Compare both versions:

> Mas viendo con el impetu que procuravan dar fin a su vida por defenderla mas a su salvo, aprovechóse de una de las pistolas que apuntó a don Rodrigo sin averle conocido, por ser la persona que mas le apretava, disparóla y no le erró, de modo que dió con el en el suelo, començando luego a pedir a vozes confession, sacó luego la otra pistola, y los criados temiendo cada uno que le hiziessen con violencia imitar a su dueño; bolvieron las espaldas a don Fadrique, y pusieronse en salvo: era esto a prima noche, y hazia obscura, con que pudo don Fadrique retirarse a su posada, seguro de que no avia sido conocido, la gente del barrio al ruido salio, aunque tarde, porque ya estava hecho el daño, hallaron a que celoso don Rodrigo rebolcandose en su sangre con las bascas de la muerte, todavia pidiendo que le confessassen, la piedad Christiana de un vezino de los que concurrieron a esto, se movio a traerle un Sacerdote, el qual pudo oirle de confession y absolverle: hecho esto acudió un Alcalde con su acompañamiento de Corchetes, que este nunca falta, y començó a hazer preguntas al herido, la passion de verse assi le hizo confessar quien le avia puesto en el ultimo trance de su vida; llevaronle con esto a su casa, donde dentro de dos horas que le hizieron la primera cura, murio cercado de toda su parentela, que eran muchos cavalleros de los principales de Sevilla. [10]

> Mais enfin, craignant de se faire tuer à force d'estre trop discret, et se voyant trop presse de Dom Diegue, il luy tira un de ses pistolets et l'entendit par terre demy-mort et demandant un Prestre à haute voix. Au bruit du coup de pistolet les braves disparutent; Dom Sanche se sauva chez luy et les voisins sortirent dans la rue et trouverent Dom Diegue, qu'ils reconneurent, tirant a la fin et qui accusa Dom Sanche de sa mort. [11]

When Dom Sanche hides in the monastery after he has killed Dom Diègue, he sends a letter to Dorotée. This letter is included

---

[10] *Ibid.*, pp. 19-20.
[11] Scarron, *op. cit.*, p. 782.

in Castillo Solórzano's version but not in Scarron's. Since they had an interview the next day, Scarron saw no purpose in including the letter. However, he does include those *billets* which he considers essential, such as the first written communication between Dorotée and Dom Sanche or the letter that Sophie left to her parents when she eloped in "Le Juge de sa propre cause." In fact, there is one letter in each of the four interpolated stories. In each case, it is an essential element. All four trigger or tell of a secret action whose outcome is related to the outcome of the *nouvelle.* In the "Histoire de l'amante invisible" a letter of the invisible lady to Dom Carlos triggers his escape from Porcia, and hence his marriage to her. In "A trompeur, trompeur et demi" the letter found by Victoria triggers her secret journey to Madrid and her marriage to Dom Fernand. In "Le Judge de sa propre cause" the letter, although it does not trigger her elopement, describes ti, and it is this letter that actually forces Dom Carlos to flee the city. Thus, here also the letter triggers an escape.

The letter in "Les deux frères rivaux" triggers a shorter journey. However, it is this journey that will set the tone for the rest of the *nouvelle,* since Dom Sanche, by going to visit Dorotée, mirrors the rest of the action which will deal with his return to Dorotée and their eventual marriage. The letter that Scarron does not include has no significance in the action, thus being an unnecessary detail. Here is the letter found in the Spanish version:

> Mi corta fortuna (dueño mio) no quiso ser igual en los medios, y fines de mi empleo, ya que me fue favorable en los principios, y assi me previno ocasion en que huviese de perder a Sevilla, y con ella todo mi gusto, la desgracia abrás sabido, y las diligencias que hazen mis contrarios para quitarme la vida tambien, deste refugio me he valido donde estoy secreto hasta poder despedirme de tus ojos, si merezco este bien, y sino la paciencia me ampare, lo que te suplico es (si te lo he merecido) que si mi ausencia durare no te olvides (bien de mi alma) de las muchas vezes que has reyterado la palabra que me as dado de ser mia, que yo te ofrezco en pago guardarte la misma fe, sino es que Dios lo ataje con el fin de mi vida, que esto podra hazer con la pena que llévo, en ausentarme de tus ojos, esto importa aora para mi seguridad, la voluntad no falte

que el tiempo acaba mayores cosas, el cielo te me guarde como desseo, tu amate, don Fadrique. [12]

Just as Scarron does not include the details of the death of Dom Diègue, he does not believe he should include the details of Dorotée's affliction when hearing of Dom Sanche's death. He only refers to her as "cette belle fille affligée." [13] Castillo Solórzano, on the other hand, states:

> Quien sintio la fingida nueva, fue la hermosa Dorotea, la qual dissimulando de dia en la presencia de su padre, por las noches eran sus ojos dos fuentes, que nunca cessavan de llorar no bastaban los consuelos de su hermosa Feliciana para que diessen alivio a su gran pena, tanto se afligio que cayó enferma en la cama de una grave melancolia que se llegaron otros achaques, con que puso en cuydado a tres doctos Medicos que la curavan, pues dudavan de su salud, que como ignoravan la causa de que procedia su mal los remedios que la aplicavan eran sin provecho, y solo servian de martirizar a la pobre señora, y no de sanarla, ella los tomava desesperada de su vida, porque acabasse mas presto con ella, y assi se lo decia a Feliciana, pero la hermosa sintiendo el verla acabar poco a poco, tomó por acuerdo amenacarla con que revelaria la causa de su mal a su anciano padre para que los medicos sabiendola la curassen con acierto. [14]

Although Scarron likes to include explanations for actions in his *nouvelle,* he restricts this to the main characters. He does not, for instance, tell us why Dom Sanche's valet, Leoncio, is not recognized by people when he returns to Sevilla. Scarron considers that since the valet was there such a short time, he does not need to explain this fact. Anyway, it is such a minor explanation that it is unnecessary to the general action of the *nouvelle* and is not included. Here is Castillo Solórzano's explanation:

> Era Leoncio poco conocido en aquella Ciudad, porque quando a su dueño le sucedio el matar a don Rodrigo, avia quatro dias solos que era llegado de Flandes a Toledo, y

---

[12] Castillo Solórzano, *op. cit.,* p. 21.
[13] Scarron, *op. cit.,* p. 785.
[14] Castillo Solórzano, *op. cit.,* p. 23.

de Toledo alli, porque se quedó a solicitar unos negocios de su dueño.[15]

Scarron, in "Le Juge de sa propre cause," had corrected María de Zayas' geography: the ship could not have landed at Fez since it was an inland city. There is no need for correction here, so Scarron, when Leoncio goes to Spain, only tells us "Dom Sanche l'envoya en Espagne."[16] Castillo Solórzano, on the other hand, tells us about his journey:

> Partiose pues de Sicilia, a Sevilla embarcandose en una buena galera que le llevó hasta Barcelona, y de alli tomo el viaje por mar hasta aquella populosa Ciudad, tesoro de las riquezas que rinden las Indias Occidentales.[17]

When Dom Sanche and Marquis Fabio decide to return to Spain, Scarron says little of the trip, while Castillo Solórzano is more specific:

> Aviendo buena ocasion de passaje de galeras se embarcaron en una, en la qual teniendo viento en favor en breve tiempo tocaron en el puerto de Barcelona, de donde tomaron la buelta de Sevilla en un navio de Genoves, alli sin sucederle estorvo en su navegacion, surgieron en pocos dias en S. Lucar, donde desembarcaron y se fueron a Sevilla.[18]

> Le Marquis Fabio et Dom Sanche s'embarquerent a Messine sur des Galeres d'Espagne qui y retournoient et arriverent heureusement a Saint-Lucar ou ils prirent la poste jusqu'a Seville.[19]

Castillo Solórzano, very interested in the mechanics of love, describes the way in which Dom Juan, Dom Sanche's brother, tries to acquire Dorotée's favor, believing that his brother is dead. Several songs are included, the music played and the instruments are described. Scarron, as he does when there is a lover's conversation,

---

[15] *Ibid.*
[16] Scarron, *op. cit.*, p. 785.
[17] Castillo Solórzano, *op. cit.*, p. 24.
[18] *Ibid.*, p. 26.
[19] Scarron, *op. cit.*, p. 786.

dismisses it in a few words. Here are both versions, not including the lengthy poems found in Castillo Solórzano:

> Aviendo templado los instrumentos (q̄ eran una harpa, dos guitarras, y un violin, a quatro vozes oyeron cantar esta letra, la qual se hizo al proposito de aver salido Dorotea aquel dia a una quinta de don Fernando de Monsalve su padre con otras damas.... Acabaron de cantar esta letra con sonoros passos de garganta, porque los musicos eran de los mas diestros q̄ avia en Sevilla.... bolvieron a cantar esta letra.... Con esta letra no menos bien cantada que la primera, dejaron la calle don Diego y los musicos. [20]

> Ils ouirent accorder des instrumens sous les fenestres de Dorotée et ensuite une excelente musique, apres laquelle une voix seule, accompagnée d'un Theorbe, se plaignit longtemps des rigeurs d'une Tygresse deguisée en Ange. [21]

A final detail that Scarron considers unnecessary: at the end of the *nouvelle,* when the triple marriage occurs, Castillo Solórzano adds the marriage of Lupercio to Andrea, Dorotée's maid. Scarron considers that this fact detracts from the main interest of the story and does not include it. Thus, the following statement in Castillo Solórzano is deleted by Scarron: "Andrea se casó con Lupercio, y la dieron grandes dádivas sus dueños con que tuvieron los dos ricos lo que vivieron." [22]

In addition to the elimination of needless details, Scarron also eliminates sententious sayings, since he considers *nouvelles* to be informal tales, and such serious moralizing, when not derived from the text itself, seems to impair the smoothness and lightness of the narrative.

One morning Dom Sanche receives the letter from Dorotée informing him that he can see her that night. Castillo Solórzano includes a general statement on the impatience of lovers. This is not present in Scarron:

---

[20] Castillo Solórzano, *op. cit.,* pp. 27-28.
[21] Scarron, *op. cit.,* p. 786.
[22] Castillo Solórzano, *op. cit.,* p. 40.

Nunca se le hizo ta largo dia como aq̄l, porq̄ siépre en los amates los puntos q̄ tardan en conseguir su deseo son dilatados siglos para ellos.[23]

When Dom Sanche finds out that people believe him to be dead, he decides to keep it that way, so as to test the resolve of Dorotée. Scarron states, with Castillo Solórzano, that it is a true test of her merit. However, Castillo Solórzano adds a general statement on the resolve or *firmeza* of women which is not present in Scarron: "Deseoso de hazer prueva de su firmeza, cosa peligrosa en mugeres, porq̄ ay muy pocas que la tengan."[24]

Castillo Solórzano includes sententious sayings when he deals with valets. Needless to say, Scarron will delete this, since it is against decorum. No matter how serious a work, a valet must act as such. Thus, the following statement is not present in Scarron. When Leoncio decides to become a monk, he does it, "desengañado de quan poco durables son los gustos desta vida."[25]

Scarron does preserve one sententious saying. However, it is more of a popular saying than a sententious saying, and does not add a serious note to the story. Here are both versions:

> Dize un adagio comun que fuego, amores, y dineros, son malos de ocultar.[26]

> On dit que l'amour, le feu et l'argent ne se peuvent longtemps cacher.[27]

This elimination of complexity in style is similar to what he has done wtih the first two stories. It was already been stated why he did not do this in "Le Juge de sa propre cause." To simplify the style, Scarron also eliminates the numerous metaphors included by Castillo Solórzano in "La confusión de una noche." When Dom Sanche goes to his rendezvous with Dorotée, he encounters the owner of the house where they are to meet. Since he had been well paid,

---

[23] *Ibid.*, pp. 15-16.
[24] *Ibid.*, p. 23.
[25] *Ibid.*, p. 24.
[26] *Ibid.*, p. 17.
[27] Scarron, *op. cit.*, p. 780.

"se ofrecia ser un mármol en el silencio."²⁸ This metaphor is not found in Scarron.

At the meeting with Dorotée, Dom Sanche is allowed to kiss her hand while Feliciana and Mariane sit close by. Castillo Solórzano describes it: "De nuevo besó don Fadrique aquel animado cristal de la mano de su hermosa dama."²⁹ Again, this is not present in Scarron. A similar metaphor had been eliminated in the "Histoire de l'amante invisible" where the invisible lady had taken off her glove to give Dom Carlos a ring while he gazed at her hand: "Descubrió un pedaço de cristal animado, que esto parecia una de sus hermosas manos."³⁰

When Dorotée finds out that Dom Sanche has drowned, she is very afflicted. Not much is said of this by Scarron, but the Spanish author states that although she seemed content in the daytime in front of her father, when she goes to her room, the picture is different. The following metaphor is not present in Scarron: "Eran sus ojos dos fuentes, que nunca cessavan de llorar."³¹

When Dom Sanche's brother comes to Sevilla and falls in love with Dorotée, Castillo Solórzano states through a metaphor that it has not been long since Dom Sanche died, and thus Dorotée, even if willing, can not favor Dom Juan. This metaphor is not present in Scarron: "Que no eran frias las cenizas de su muerto galan."³²

When Dom Sanche arrives in Sevilla, he discovers that another man is courting Dorotée. As he stands back and listens to his serenade, he becomes very jealous. This is described by Castillo Solórzano through a metaphor: "le abrasavan los celos."³³

Dorotée, knowing that her sister Felicianne is in love with Dom Juan, the man that is courting her, says a few detrimental things about him to see how her sister will react, and to make sure that she is in love with him. These phrases by Dorotée hurt Felicianne. Castillo Solórzano tells us this through a metaphor which is not found in Scarron. These arrows can be compared to the arrows of love that also pierce her heart:

---

²⁸ Castillo Solórzano, *op. cit.*, p. 16.
²⁹ *Ibid.*, p. 17.
³⁰ *Ibid.*, p. 65.
³¹ *Ibid.*, p. 23.
³² *Ibid.*, p. 25.
³³ *Ibid.*, p. 27.

124 THE INTERPOLATED STORIES IN THE "ROMAN COMIQUE"

> Cada razon destas endereçadas a su empleo eran para Feliciana saetas que le rompian el coraçon porque como amava tiernamente a don Diego, sentia que su hermosa hermana dixesse esto.[34]

When Andrea, thinking it was Dom Juan who she had left in the garden, leads Dom Sanche instead to the lighted room where Dorotée is waiting with her sister, and the mistake is discovered, Castillo Solórzano describes, through metaphor, the amazement of Dom Sanche and of Andrea, who thinks he is a ghost; Scarron does not:

> Entró pues donde estavan las dos beldades muy descuydadas de lo que vieron, pues luego que Dorotea vio a don Fadrique, con el susto que podreys considerar de quien le jusgava muerto, se quedó sin sentido, procuró su hermana q̄ bolviesse en si; estando a todo esto don Fadrique hecho un marmol, y Andrea hecha un yelo, imaginando venia de la otra vida ofendido de Dorotea.[35]

> Dom Sanche entra donc où estoient les deux belles sœurs qui furent bien surprises de le voir. Dorotée en demeura sans sentiment, comme un personne morte, et, si sa sœur ne l'eus soutenue et ne l'eust mise dans une chaise, elle seroit tombée de sa hauteur. Dom Sanche demeura immobil; Isabelle pensa mourir de peur et crut que Dom Sanche mort leur apparoissoit pour venger le tort que luy faisoit sa Maistresse.[36]

In addition to metaphors, there are other complexities of style which are present in the Spanish story and which Scarron eliminates, to produce a clear, simple, and straightforward narrative. Castillo Solórzano, as María de Zayas in el "Juez de su causa," includes many mythological allusions in his story. For example, when Dom Sanche goes to church and finds himself standing close to Dorotée, Scarron states: "Dom Sanche se trouva par hazard entre les deux belles Souers."[37] Castillo Solórzano does not believe this to be a chance

---

[34] *Ibid.*, p. 29.
[35] *Ibid.*, p. 35.
[36] Scarron, *op. cit.*, p. 790.
[37] *Ibid.*, p. 774.

meeting, but a prearranged event, stemming from the kingdom of Love. Here is what he says:

> Al fin hizieron su assistencia en la parte donde estava Dorotea, que amor compadecido della lo devió de permitir, para aumentar vassallos a su dilatada Monarchia. [38]

Dom Diègue, an admirer of Dorotée, was afraid that she was in love with another, and thus stood guard on her street. This is described by Castillo Solórzano with a mythological allusion which is absent from the French version:

> Este cavallero viendo que ni papel suyo podia hazer que le admitiesse, viendo que su esquivez para con el era muy grande, y que se podia dignar por sangre y de mas partes, que en el cocurrian, de que la sirviesse, no lo hazia, dio en tener sospecha que esta dama tenia secreto algun empleo amoroso, afligiale esta sospecha, y por salir de ella, dio en ser vigilante Argos de noche y de dia de su calle. [39]

This metaphor is followed up by the story. Argos was a mythological being with many eyes placed so as to watch over a lady that did not belong to him. He was finally slain by Mercury. Dom Diègue is then this being trying to guard over Dorotée who does not belong to him. He must be, and is killed by Mercury, Dom Sanche, thus freeing Dorotée. This is the one act of retributive justice that occurs in the story. Although Dom Sanche was seeking justice through this act, he must still alone for it, since it was murder. His journey to Naples and then his battle with the Turks is an expiation, since he performed as act reserved for the gods. Scarron passes over this event, since his version deals mainly with the final order achieved when all things are in harmony, and when authority is just.

As soon as Dom Sanche arrives in Madrid, he worries that the day is taking too long and wants the chariot of the sun to conclude its journey so that he may go see his beloved hiding in the darkness of the night. Needless to say, this is not present in Scarron:

---

[38] Castillo Solórzano, *op. cit.*, p. 11.
[39] *Ibid.*, p. 17.

> El dia siguiente lo pasó con no poca impaciencia desseando que escondiesse Febo sus rayos para dar lugar que las tinieblas de la noche le ocultassen con cuyo favor esperava encubierto ver las paredes de la casa de su dama. [40]

In discussing how long the interval seems for lovers between their rendezvous with their beloved, and how short the time they are together, Castillo Solórzano uses hyperbole. This is absent from Scarron. Speaking of the rendezvous with Dorotée, Dom Sanche wants that "durara aquel breve rato dilatados siglos." [41]

As in all previous stories, many specific details mentioned by Castillo Solórzano are changed to generalities in the French version. This increases the classical texture of the work, since Clacissism prefers to deal in generalities. For example, speaking of Dom Diègue, as a good suitor for Dorotée, Castillo Solórzano states:

> Entre los pretendientes desta dama avia un cavallero llamado don Rodrigo de Ribera bizarro, galan, y con un Mayorazgo de tres mil ducados de renta. [42]

Scarron considers that the exact amount of money is not necessary; he only places him in a category:

> Ce rival de Dom Sanche estoit riche, de bonne maison et estoit agreable a Dom Manuel qui ne pressoit pourtant pas sa fille de l'épouser. [43]

When Dom Sanche kills Dom Diegue, he finds out that the law is looking for him, and also that Dom Diegue's relatives want revenge. He decides to hide in a Monastery. Scarron mentions this: "Il se retira donc dans un Couvent, d'où il fit sçavoir de ses nouvelles a Dorotée." [44] The Spanish version states in addition which monastery and of what order it was: "Se fue al Monasterio de las Cuevas (Ordé de la Cartuja) donde secretamente se retiro bien apas-

---

[40] *Ibid.*, p. 26.
[41] *Ibid.*, p. 17.
[42] *Ibid.*
[43] Scarron, *op. cit.*, p. 780.
[44] *Ibid.*, p. 782.

sionado de que le huviesse sucedido esto en tiepo q̃ tan adelante estava en sus amores." [45]

Dom Sanche remains in that monastery for a few days until he believes it is safe to leave. After saying farewell to Dorotée, he leaves Sevilla disguised. The Spanish version mentions the type of disguise while Scarron considers that the only fact necessary for the story is that he is disguised, and not what his disguise is. Thus, the general statement suffices, while Castillo Solórzano must mention a specific one:

> Partio del Convento en habito de Religioso, dejando escrito a su padre a Indias, encomendada la carta al agente que en Sevilla tenia. [46]

> Il sortit deguisé de Seville et laissa, devant que de partir, des lettres au facteur de son Pere pour les luy faire tenir aux Indes. [47]

As in "A trompeur, trompeur et demi," Scarron is reluctant to mention a specific hour for a rendezvous. He states only whether it is night or day, considering the particular hour a needless detail. When Dom Sanche, accompanied by his valet and by Marquis Fabio, goes to Dorotée's street, Castillo Solórzano states:

> Serian las onze de la noche, que aunque pudieron yr mas temprano estavale mejor al intento de don Fadrique ser aquella sazon, pues llegó en ocasion q̃ hallaron en la calle gente. [48]

Scarron only says: "La nuict, Dom Sanche et le Marquis Fabio allerent faire la ronde dans le quartier de Dom Manuel." [49] We can see the same type of change from the specific to the general in another instance where time is involved. Dom Juan was to meet Dorotée in the garden at midnight according to Castillo Solórzano:

> Aguardava hora este cavallero para yr a verse con la dama, y esta era la de media noche, pero como el relox de los

---

[45] Castillo Solórzano, *op. cit.*, p. 20.
[46] *Ibid.*, p. 21.
[47] Scarron, *op. cit.*, p. 783.
[48] Castillo Solórzano, *op. cit.*, p. 26.
[49] Scarron, *op. cit.*, p. 786.

amantes anda siempre antojado como lo piden sus desseos, media hora antes llego al jardin. [50]

Notice how this metaphor agrees with the sententious saying dealing with the impatience of lovers that Scarron also eliminated. The French author only states here: Cependant Dom Juan vint à l'heure qu'on luy avoit donnée." [51]

These, then, are the changes made by Scarron to make his version agree with the French classical tradition. There are, however, many other changes. For example, Scarron changes many of the names of characters in the story. Dom Sanche's valet is called Sanchez by Scarron. This similarity of names serves to point out the close relationship that exists between them. This has already been discussed previously, when they were compared to a knight and his squire. Castillo Solórzano calls Sanchez Leoncio, while Dom Sanche is called don Fadrique de Silva. Dom Sanche's first rival, Dom Diègue according to Scarron, is really don Rodrigo de Rivera, while Scarron's Dom Juan is actually don Diego in the Spanish version. This mix up in names and the fact that Scarron calls the wrong person Dom Diègue while stating that he seems to remember that this is his name, might seem to point out that Scarron did not have the original Spanish version in front of him while he wrote his story. There are even some other changes in names: Andrea, Dorotée's maid, is called Isabelle by Scarron; and Lupercio, Dom Diègue's valet is called Gusman by the French author.

These changes in name, and the way in which Scarron states that he seems to remember a name, should not make us believe that he did not have the original text in front of him while he adapted it. There are too many similarities of detail for this to be true. When Dom Sanche is speaking to Dorotée in church without knowing who she is, he compares her to Dorotée herself. She answers by asking him if he has heard whether Dorotée prefers any man in particular. In both versions, Dom Sanche answers that he does not care since he does not merit her:

---

[50] Castillo Solórzano, *op. cit.*, p. 34.
[51] Scarron, *op. cit.*, p. 790.

> No lo merezco quanto a lo primero dixo el, y quanto a lo segundo fuera locura mia pensar que lo que tantos tienen granjeado un forastero se lo podria quitar.[52]

> Comme je me suis veu fort eloigné de la meriter, luy dit Dom Sanche, je ne me suis pas beaucoup mis en peine de m'informer de ce que vous dites.[53]

Also, in both versions, Dorotée replies in the same manner to Dom Sanche's statement that he does not merit her. This discussion of merit mirrors his future adventures, which certainly earn him her hand. Here are both versions:

> Mirad señor dixo ella, los caprichos de las mugeres son extraordinarios, no desconfieys que ta vez suele un rezien venido caer mas en gracia que quantos naturales esten obligando.[54]

> Le caprice des Dames est quelquefois estrange et, souvent, le premier abord d'un nouveau venu fait plus de progrez que plusieurs annees de service des galans qui sont tous les jours devant leurs yeux.[55]

Notice how this statement found in both versions seems to agree with the thoughts of Castillo Solórzano and Scarron since in three of the four stories it is a stranger that makes a beautiful woman fall in love: Dom Carlos, Dom Fernand, and now Dom Sanche.

In the same conversation at the church, Dorotée, her face masked, tells Dom Sanche that even though he admires her cleverness, he would not admire her beauty so much. In both versions, Dom Sanche gives a very witty answer:

> Infiero que soys muy hermosa, porque ningun viviente dessea desacreditarse assi, antes esforçar su partido de todas maneras.[56]

> Ha! vous ne pouvez estre que fort belle, repliqua Dom Sanche, puisque vous avouez si franchement que vous ne

---

[52] Castillo Solórzano, *op. cit.*, p. 13.
[53] Scarron, *op. cit.*, p. 775.
[54] Castillo Solórzano, *op. cit.*, p. 13.
[55] Scarron, *op. cit.*, p. 775.
[56] Castillo Solórzano, *op. cit.*, p. 13.

l'estes pas et je ne doute plus à cette heure que vous ne vous vouliez defaire de moy. [57]

Dorotée then asks Dom Sanche to tell her about himself. In both versions he states that his last name is that of his mother, that his father is governor of Peru, and that he has won the order of St. James in Flanders:

> Y assi cumpliendo con vuestro mandato digo que mi patria es Toledo, mi nombre don Fadrique de Silva, tomando el apellido de mi madre. Tego a mi padre (que ya es viudo) en el Pyru Governador de Quito, mi profession hasta aora a sido la de soldado he militado en Napoles y despues en Flandes, aviendo mis servicios llegado al puesto de Coronel y ser encomendado en la orden de Santiago. [58]

> Sçachez donc, aymable inconnue, luy dit-il, que je porte le nom de Sylva qui est celuy de ma mere, que mon Pere est gouverneur de Quito dans le Perou, que je suis dans Seville par son ordre, et que j'ay passé toute ma vie en Flandres où j'ay merité des plus beaux employs de l'armee et une Commanderie de Sain-Jacques. [59]

When Dorotée's father, Dom Manuel, asked her to decide about a husband she tells him in both versions that she is too young to marry:

> Suplicando a su padre no tratasse de casarla tan presto, porque era en tan poca edad ponerla en mucho cuydado, y sugeción. [60]

> Dom Manuel qui ne pressoit pourtant pas sa fille de l'épouser à cause que, toutes les fois qu'il luy enparloit elle le conjuroit de ne la marier pas si jeune. [61]

All these similarities point to the fact that Scarron had the Spanish text in front of him when he wrote his French version. Also, he follows the structure of the Spanish story point by point. That is,

---

[57] Scarron, *op. cit.*, p. 776.
[58] Castillo Solórzano, *op. cit.*, p. 14.
[59] Scarron, *op. cit.*, p. 776.
[60] Castillo Solórzano, *op. cit.*, p. 17.
[61] Scarron, *op. cit.*, p. 780.

he presents it in chronological order. As seen in "A trompeur, trompeur et demi" and even in "Le Juge de sa propre cause," this is not the way he likes to write his tales, since he prefers to begin them *in medias res* so as to arouse the reader's interest. He then fills in the rest with *récits*. Here, he has taken the Spanish story of simple construction and followed it, while he could have started it, in the manner of the other stories, at a point of great interest, such as the battle with the Turkish fleet where he jumps into the ocean before being captured.

There are many additions made by Scarron to the Spanish text and these fall in several categories. First, as in all other stories, Scarron adds explanations when he thinks the Spanish version is not clear enough. Castillo Solórzano describes in a very few lines how Dom Sanche, after having jumped into the ocean, found himself at a fisherman's house in Sicily. Scarron knows that the fact that Dom Sanche swam one and a half miles in the midst of a storm, and finally found himself on the rugged coast of Sicily deserves more than a couple of lines, because first he must explain how Dom Sanche did it, and second he must give details of such an exciting adventure. Although this was not exactly a shipwreck, it is in the same tradition, and reminds the reader of the many shipwrecks that occur in the heroic novels of the time particularly the ones of Mlle de Scudéry and of Gomberville. Scarron, then, is adding here detailed description to increase the novelesque appeal of his *nouvelle*. In "Le Juge de sa propre cause" he did this constantly. Compare the Spanish version to the French version where Scarron has made this episode into an adventure fit for a seventeenth-century novel:

> Se arrojó al mar donde a nado, pudo con buen aliento nadar hasta tomar puerto en una calavecina del puerto de Messina, y aquella noche durmio en casa de un pescador que piadoso le albergó compadecido de su fortuna. [62]

> Se lança dans la mer, esperant en quelque façon, comme il estoit grand nageur, de gagner à la nage les Galeres Chrestiennes, mais le mauvais temps empescha qu'il n'en fust apperceu, quoyque le general Chrestien, qui avoit esté témoin de l'action de Dom Sanche et qui se desesperoit de

---

[62] Castillo Solórzano, *op. cit.*, p. 22.

> sa perte qu'il croyoit inevitable, fist revirer sa Galere du costé qu'il s'estoit jetté dans la mer. Dom Sanche cependant, fendoit les vagues de toute la force de ses bras et, aprés avoir nagé quelque temps vers la terre, où le vent et la marée le portoient, il trouva hereusement une planche de Galeres Turques que le canon avoit brisées et se servit utilement de ces secours venu à propos qu'il crut que le Ciel luy avoit envoyé. Il n'y avoit pas plus d'une lieue et demie du lieu où le combat s'estoit fait jusqu'a la coste de Sicile et Dom Sanche y aborda plus viste qu'il ne l'esperoit, aydé, comme il estoit, du vent et de la marée. Il prit terre sans se blesser contre le rivage et, apres avoir remercié Dieu de l'avoir tiré d'un peril si evident, il alla plus avant en terre, autant que sa lassitude le pût permettre; et d'une eminence qu'il monta apperceut un hameau habité de Pécheurs qu'il trouva les plus charitables du monde. Les efforts qu'il avoit faits pendant le combat, qui l'avoient fort echauffé, et ceux qu'il avoit faits dans la mer et le froid qu'il avoit suffert, et en-suitte dans ses habits mouillez, luy causent une violente fiévre qui lui fit longtemps garder le lit. [63]

As Dom Sanche arrives on shore and is taken to the house of the fisherman, he should realize that people will consider him dead, so he should let it be known who he is. Castillo Solórzano does not explain why Dom Sanche stayed at the fisherman's cottage without revealing his name or making any effort to get in touch with his acquaintances. It is true, however, that soon he hits upon the idea of letting others believe he is dead so he can safely return to Sevilla, and he can test faithfulness of Dorotée. However, his initial reluctance to declare himself alive is not explained. Scarron has to add an explanation, which is that he became ill after such an adventure:

> Mais enfin il guerit sans y faire autre chose que de vivre de regime. Pendant sa maladie, il fit dessein de laisser tout le monde dans la croyance qu'on devoit avoir de sa mort pour n'avoir plus tant à se garder de ses ennemis les parens de Dom Diegue et pour esprouver la fidelité de Dorotée. [64]

Related to these explanations is the concept of motivation. While the Spanish author is mainly concerned with plot and an obvious

---

[63] Scarron, op. cit., p. 784.
[64] Ibid.

didacticism, Scarron desires to explain human action. This again is an integral part of classicism, leading to the writings of Jean Racine and Mme de La Fayette. For example, in Castillo Solórzano, Andrea just tells Lupercio what she knows about the love of her mistress with Dom Sanche, no explanation being given for such gossip in a trusted servant. Scarron adds a motive. He has the meeting take place in the house of Marine, an old servant of Dorotée. He then adds envy as a motive, since Isabelle (Andrea) has always been envious of Dorotée's confidence in Marine. Later, Scarron adds that Isabelle is also envious because of all the money Marine is making in the affair. This will be discussed later when humor is considered. Here is what Scarron states about Isabelle's relation to Marine.

> Isabelle avoit bien du deplaisir de ce que Marine, la femme du Chirurgien chez qui Dorotée et Dom Sanche se voyoient secretement, et qui avoit servy sa maistresse devant elle, estoit encore sa confidente dans un affaire de cette nature où la liberalité d'un Amant se faisoit toujours paroistre. Elle avoit eu connoissance de la chaîne d'or que Dom Sanche avoit donnée a Marine, de plusieurs autres presens qu'il luy avoit faits et s'imaginoist qu'elle en avoit receu bien d'autres. Elle en haissoit Marine.... [65]

Returning to the naval battle, Castillo Solórzano, in his description of the fight mentions that Dom Sanche leaped into an enemy ship and fought there with many of his companions; and when the ship suddenly separated, he jumped into the water before being captured. This short description is filled with fallacies that Scarron tries to explain in his version. In the first place, if Dom Sanche was in the enemy ship with many of his companions, why did he not help them fight instead of jumping into the water? Second, why did the Spanish ship not come back again and try to approach the Turkish ship? And finally, why were the ships separated in the first place? Scarron introduces a storm. It was the storm that caused the ships to separate, and prevented them from coming together again. Also, Dom Sanche leaped alone into the enemy ship, and was not followed by the Spanish sailors, who were fearful of the storm.

---

[65] *Ibid.*, p. 781.

Thus, finding himself alone, he leaped into the water rather than being captured. Here are both versions:

> Acertó don Fadrique (aserrandose las capitanas) a saltar en la contraria donde peleó valientemente a vista de su General, mas aviendose desaferrado se pusieron los enemigos en huyda; esto visto por nuestro esforçado cavallero, y que era fuerça llevarle cautivo, tomando la espada en la boca se arrojó al mar. [66]

> La Patronne des Galeres Chrestiennes s'estoit attachée à celle des Turcs qui, pour estre mieux armée que les autres, avoit fait aussi plus de resistance. La mer cependant estoit devenue grosse et l'orage s'estoit augmenté si furieusement qu'enfin les Chrestiens et les Turcs songerent moins à s'entre-nuire qu'à se garentir de l'orage. On déprit donc de part de d'autre les crampons de fer dont les Galeres avoient esté accrochées et la Patronne Turque s'éloigna de la Chrestienne dans le temps que le trop hardy Dom Sanche s'estoit jetté dedans et n'avoit esté suivy de personne. [67]

This incident must have reminded Scarron, as he wrote, it of Mlle de Scudéry's novel, *Le Grand Cyrus* where Artamène and the turkis pirates exchange ships. However, more important, since Cervantes' *Don Quijote de la Mancha* has been proven to be a decisive influence in the *Roman comique,* the similarity of this passage to one in the famous Spanish novel should be pointed out. In the story of the *cautivo,* already mentioned in connection to "Le Juge de sa propre cause," Cervantes has a similar adventure where a Spanish soldier is captured by the enemy because he was alone on the ship. He does not however leap into the ocean. Castillo Solórzano may have had this passage in mind, and Scarron may have been reminded of it:

> En aquel día, digo, donde quedó el orgullo y la soberbia otamana quebrantada, entre tantos venturosos que allí hubo (porque más ventura tuvieron los cristianos que allí murieron que los que vivos y vencedores quedaron), yo solo fui el desdichado; pues en cambio de que pudiera esperar, si fuera en los romanos siglos, alguna naval corona, me vi

---

[66] Castillo Solórzano, *op. cit.,* p. 22.
[67] Scarron, *op. cit.,* p. 783.

> aquella noche que siguió a tan famoso día con cadenas a los pies y esposas a las manos. Y fue desta suerte: que habiendo el Uchalí, rey de Argel, atrevido y venturoso corsario, embestido y rendido la capitana de Malta, que solo tres caballeros quedaron vivos en ella, y estos mal heridos, acudió la capitana de Juan Andrea a socorrella, en la cual y iba con mi compañía; y haciendo lo que debía en ocasión semejante, salté en la galera contraria, la cual, desviándose de la que la habia enbestido, estorbó que mis soldados me siguiesen, y así, me hallé solo entre mis enemigos, a quien no pude resistir por ser tantos; en fin me rindieron lleno de heridas. [68]

Scarron, as he did in the other interpolated stories, likes to add explanations dealing with Spanish customs. For example, discussing why Spanish women often look out their windows, and why many shows are put on the streets of the city, Scarron explains:

> Mais si leur merite leur causoit tant de fatigue dans les lieux publics et dans les Eglises, il leur attiroit souvent, devant les fenestres de la maison de leur Pere, des divertissemens qui leur rendoient supportable la severe closture à quoy les obligeoient leur sexe et la coustume de la Nation. [69]

Later, when Dom Sanche meets Dorotée in church, he need not comment on this rendezvous in a sacred place, since he has already done so in the "Histoire de l'amante invisible":

> On prophane les Eglises en ce pays-là aussi bien qu'au nôtre, et le Temple de Dieu sert de rendez-vous aux godelureaux et aux coquettes, à la honte de ceux qui ont la maudite ambition d'achallander leurs Eglises et de s'oster la pratique les uns aux otres; on y devoit donner ordre et établir des chasse-godelureaux et de chasse-coquettes dans les eglises, comme des chasse-chiens et des chasse-chiennes. [70]

---

[68] Miguel de Cervantes, *Don Quijote de la Mancha,* Martín de Riquer, ed. (Barcelona: Editorial Juventud, S. A., 1967), pp. 398-399.
[69] Scarron, *op. cit.,* p. 773.
[70] *Ibid.,* p. 552.

However, Scarron does explain why Dorotée was not insulted when Dom Sanche expressed his love for her. He attributes her acceptance to the fact that the Spanish act thusly:

> Quelques Dames tristes, de celles qui sont tôujours en peine de la conduite des autres et fort en repos de la leur, qui se font elles-mesmes Arbitres du mal et du bien, quoy-qu'on puisse faire des gageures sur leur vertu comme sur tout ce qui n'est pas bien averé, et qui croyent qu'avec un peu de rudesse brutalle et de grimace devote elles ont de l'honneur à revendre, quoy-que l'enjouement de leur jeunesse ait esté plus scandaleux que le chagrin de leurs rides n'a esté de bon example, ces Dames donc, le plus souvent de connoissance tres-courte, diront icy que Mademoiselle Dorotée est pour le moins une étourdie, non seulement d'avoir si brusquement fait de si grandes avances à un homme qu'elle ne connoissoit que de veue, mais aussi d'avoir souffert qu'on luy parlast d'amour; et que si une fille sur qui elles auroient pouvoir en avoit fait autant, elle ne seroit pas un quart d'heure dans le monde. Mais que les ignorantes sçachent que chaque pays a ses coustumes particulieres et que, si, en France, les femmes et mesmes les filles qui vont partout sur leur bonne foy, s'offencent, ou du moins le doivent faire, de la moindre declaration d'amour, qu'en Espagne, où elles sont reserrées comme des Religieuses, on ne les offence point de leur dire qu'on les ayme, quand celuy qui leur diroit n'auroit pas de quoy se faire aymer. Elles font bien davantage: ce son tôujours presque les Dames qui font les premiers avances et qui sont les premieres prises parce qu'elles sont les dernieres à estre veues des Galans qu'elles voyent tous les jours dans les Eglises, dans le Cours et de leurs Balcons et jalousies.[71]

Some additions by Scarron increase the informality or create humor in the story so as to increase the lightness of the narrative. The humor in this story contains nothing of the satire present in the "Histoire de l'amante invisible" since here Scarron is trying to get a point across and not satirize a position. Also, the humor in this story contrasts with the seriousness of the second and third stories. While they presented a conflict, this story presents a resolution and thus the lightness of touch agrees with the tone of the story.

---

[71] *Ibid.*, pp. 776-777.

After the first rendezvous of the lovers, Scarron adds that many messages were sent back and forth expressing their love. However, he regrets to point out that he does not have in his possession any of these *billets*. Such a statement adds a certain lightness and informality to the narrative: "Je ne vous feray point voir icy de leurs Billets amoureux, car il n'en est point tombé entre mes mains." [72]

When Scarron mentions that Dorotée has another admirer and thus Dom Sanche has a rival, the French author adds in passing: "Je me viens de souvenir qu'il s'appelloit Dom Diègue." [73]

Again, the description of Dom Diègue's valet, Guzmán, is humorous and adds a lightness to the story. Compare this description with Castillo Solórzano's:

> Moço de buen talle, musico y con puntas de poeta. [74]

> Ce vallet se nommoit Gusman et, ayant du Ciel une demy-teinture de Poésie, faisoit la pluspart des Romances de Seville, ce qui est à Paris des chansons de Pont-Neuf; il les chantoit sur sa guitere et ne les chantoit pas toutes unies et sans y faire de la broderie des levres ou de la langue. Il dançoit la sarabande, n'estoit jamais sans castagnettes, avoit eu envie d'estre Comedien et faisoit enter dans la composition de mon merite quelque bravoure, mais, pour vous dire les choses comme elles sont, un peu filouttiere. Tous ces beaux talens, joints à quelque eloquence de memoire que luy avoit communiquée celle de son maistre, l'avoient rendu sans contredit le blanc (si je l'ose ainsi dire) de tous les desirs emoureux des servantes qui se croyoient aymables. [75]

Isabelle, the maid of Dorotée, is upset not just because she is envious of Marine, but also because Marine is receiving all the money. Scarron then goes on to say that this may lead one to believe Isabelle is somewhat concerned with money. Such an understatement adds humor to the tale: "C'est ce qui m'a fait croire que la belle fille estoit un peu interessée." [76]

---

[72] *Ibid.*, p. 780.
[73] *Ibid.*
[74] Castillo Solórzano, *op. cit.*, p. 18.
[75] Scarron, *op. cit.*, pp. 780-781.
[76] *Ibid.*, p. 781.

Finally, Scarron keeps the one passage in Castillo Solórzano that can be described as humorous. Here are both versions:

> Estando a todo esto don Fadrique hecho un marmol y Andrea hecho un yelo imaginando venia de la otra vida ofendido de lo que avia aquella noche. [77]

> Isabelle pensa mourir de peur et crut que Dom Sanche mort leur apparoissoit pour venger le tort que luy faisoit sa Maistresse. [78]

Notice that a great deal of the humor in the story is derived from the servants. This reflects Scarron's dramatic technique in which valets produce comic relief much like the *gracioso* in the Spanish *Comedia*. This is understandable since many of his plays have Spanish sources. One for example, *L'Heritier ridicule*, written in 1649, is based on the one play included in Castillo Solórzano's *Los alivios de Casandra*: *El mayorazgo figura*.

Although Scarron eliminated many metaphors present in the Spanish story, he adds many similes that are not present in Castillo Solórzano's story. For example, when Dom Sanche is talking to Dorotée in the church, he adds figures of speech to embellish his language and thus finds a more "poetical" expression of his feelings:

> J'estimeray toûjors tout ce qui me viendra de vous comme s'il me venoit du Ciel, luy dit le passionné Dom Sanche. [79]

Later, when Dom Sanche goes to a rendezvous with Dorotée, Dom Diègue is waiting for him, accompanied by two *braves*. Dom Sanche must defend himself from this jealous man. Scarron described the defense with a simile: "Il se deffendit d'abord comme un Lyon." [80]

When Dom Sanche returns to Madrid to see Dorotée he finds that there is music at her window, and the song "se plaignit longtemps des rigueurs d'un Tygresse deguisée en Ange." [81] This is a

---

[77] Castillo Solórzano, *op. cit.*, p. 35.
[78] Scarron, *op. cit.*, p. 790.
[79] *Ibid.*, p. 779.
[80] *Ibid.*, p. 782.
[81] *Ibid.*, p. 786.

metaphor used to substitute for Castillo Solórzano's comparison of Dorotée with a shepherdess which does not fit the events of the story.

Scarron even adds a poem which is lacking in the Spanish version:

> Ils se dirent en peu de temps
> Tout ce que l'amour nous fait dire
> Quand il est maistre de nos sens. [82]

However, most of these additions are in good taste and are not as *précieux* as the embellishments found in Castillo Solórzano. Other than these additions, there are other changes which can be seen in Scarron. For example, some of these changes are made in order to simplify the story. In the Spanish version, Dorotée sees Dom Sanche riding his horse in front of her window. It is at this point that she falls in love with him. Castillo Solórzano describes how she spends the night just thinking of him, and how finally, the next morning, she goes to church to meet him. The French version is very different. Scarron simplifies and shortens the tale by not stating that Dorotée had seen Dom Sanche that day on his horse. Thus, their first meeting is at the church and there is no description of her feelings that night. [83] This simplification also serves another purpose. In the French story it is not Dorotée then that falls in love with Dom Sanche and tries to meet him. Scarron has love begin simultaneously at a mutual encounter. Scarron presents love as he thinks it should be: an interrelation of two people grounded on reality and based on *estime*. Scarron satirized Dom Carlos in the "Histoire de l'amante invisible" for not knowing what he wanted. He has also satirized Ragotin. Both love through their imaginations and are thus led by women whom they do not really know. In "A trompeur, trompeur et demi" the hero is criticized for not knowing what he wants, and it is Victoria who must correct the situation. Sophie in "Le Juge de sa propre cause" must also correct the situation. The only relationship wehe the man is dominant is that of Destin and Estoile. Now that they are triumphant and have

---

[82] *Ibid.*, p. 779.
[83] Castillo Solórzano, *op. cit.*, p. 10.

attained justice, it is only fitting that this story mirror their concept of love, and place such an afection in its proper perspective.

No longer are we dealing with the idealized love of a knight as stated before, but a love based on reality and order. Thus, Scarron must change the beginning of the Spanish story so as to place love in its proper perspective.

Scarron also simplifies the Spanish version by changing the meeting place. Castillo Solórzano, as an author of complex *novelas* in plot, adds confusing details as to the place of the rendezvous. Scarron is more straightforward. Here are both versions:

> Y trataron el modo como poder favorecer a este galan con secreto, el que Feliciana le dio fue, que pues desde su casa avia passadiço para otra en que vivia una señora viuda deuda suya se declarasse co ella, y alli fuesse llamado don Fadrique a verse con Dorotea, no salio a esto la dama, viendo que la assistencia de Fadrique de dia en su calle luego que fuesse favorecido haria publico su amor, porque en ella assistian otros cavalleros que la pretendian, y avia de ser visto dellos, yy conocido su empleo; avia otra casa de un pobre Oficial junta a esta del passadiço, y alli quiso que se hisiesse una puertecilla secreta donde Dorotea saliesse en verse con Fadrique, mas su entrada alli avia de ser por una puerta falsa que cahia a otra calle, que con esto desmentian sospechas y atajavan presunciones. [84]

> Mais Feliciane, qui estoit heureuse a trouver des expediens, fit souvenir sa sœur qu'une Dame de leurs parentes et de plus de leurs intimes amies (car toutes les parentes n'en sont pas), la serviroit de tout son cœur dans une affaire où il y alloit de son repos. Vous sçavez bien, luy disoit cette bonne sœur, la plus commode du monde, que Marine qui nous a servies si longtemps est mariée à un Chirurgien qui loue de nostre parente une petite maison jointe à la sienne et que les deux maisons ont une entrée l'une dans l'autre. Elles sont dans un quartier éloigné et quand on remarqueroit que nous irions visiter nostre Parente plus souvent que nous n'aurions jamais fait, on ne prendra pas garde de ce Dom Sanche entre chez un Chirurgien. [85]

---

[84] *Ibid.*, p. 15.
[85] Scarron, op. cit., p. 778.

Other changes are made by Scarron to increase *vraisemblance*. For example, several times he diminishes the number of the enemy. When Dom Sanche fights Dom Diègue in front of Dorotée's house, Castillo Solórzano states that he must fight four people, [86] while Scarron reduces the number to three to make Dom Sanche's victory appear more plausible. [87] Then, when the Spanish galleys discover the Turkish ships, Castillo Solórzano states that the Spanish sink twelve enemy ships [88] while Scarron states that there were only eight ships to start with, and that only three were sunk. [89] This makes the battle more *vraisemblable*.

When Dom Juan has songs sung for Dorotée, the Spanish version presents pastoral poems declaring the love of shepherdes Dorinda (Dorotée) for a shepherd Dom Juan. This is not in keeping with their relationship, since she has been ignoring him. It is more *vraisemblable* to state what Scarron mentions the song are about: "des rigueurs d'une Tygresse deguisée en Ange." [90]

As in the other three stories, Scarron changes the Spanish version in order to make the women stronger. What is significant in this story is that he does not. In fact, as stated before he eliminates the one paragraph that appears to make Dorotée the dominant character in the relationship. This must be pointer out, since the meaning of this story is tied to the fact that woman has gone back to her proper place, once the man finds out what love is, and does not confuse it with an ideal.

Man in this story has also found the meaning of justice, and the actions of all the main characters are based on reason. For example, in Castillo Solórzano, the lovers must part because Dorotée's father has arrived. In Scarron, the reason given is that the time set aside for this rendezvous is over. Thus, in Castillo Solórzano they are afraid of justice, while in Scarron they act through reason and order. Here are both versions:

---

[86] Castillo Solórzano, *op. cit.*, p. 19.
[87] Scarron, *op. cit.*, p. 782.
[88] Castillo Solórzano, *op. cit.*, p. 22.
[89] Scarron, *op. cit.*, p. 783.
[90] *Ibid.*, p. 786.

> Pero siendo avisadas que avia venido su anciano padre fue fuerça la despedida; bien cotra la voluntad de los dos amantes. [91]

> Et Marine les fit souvenir de se separer quand il en fut temps. [92]

Don Sanche, in Castillo Solórzano, falls in love with Dorotée because fo her beauty. [93] In Scarron, he praises her esprit, which is how love should begin. [94] A statement by Mme de Lafayette could be applied here:

> Il parut aux yeux de tout le monde qu'ils avoient l'un pour l'autre cet agrement qui precede d'ordinaire les grandes passions. [95]

Scarron even adds moralizing through a speech made by Dorotée. It is a speech that reconciles order and obedience with justice and love. It is this reconciliation which is the theme of the story and of the *Roman comique*.

> Pour moy, disoit Dorotée à sa sœur, je suis bien asseurée que l'amour ne me fera jamais rien faire contre mon devoir, mais je suis aussi bien resolue de ne me marier jamais avec un homme qui ne possedera pas luy seul tout ce que j'aurois a chercher en plusieurs autres et j'ayme bien mieux passer ma vie dans un Convent qu'avec un marry que je ne pourrois pas aymer. [96]

This realization that man must strive for what he wants within the limits of society is an essential thought in the novel. Sometimes authority in the name of society acts against justice. This is why obedience and justice are sometimes in opposition. In "Le Juge de sa propre cause" Sophie wanted justice, but it was denied by her father's authority. Here, authority understands the meaning of justice.

---

[91] Castillo Solórzano, *op. cit.*, p. 16.
[92] Scarron, *op. cit.*, p. 779.
[93] Castillo Solórzano, *op. cit.*, p. 13.
[94] Scarron, *op. cit.*, p. 775.
[95] Marie Madeleine comtesse de La Fayette, *Histoire de Madame Henriette d'Angleterre* (Paris: F. Rieders et Cie, éditeurs, 1925), p. 87.
[96] Scarron, *op. cit.*, p. 777.

Dorotée's father states: "Don Manuel se mit au milieu d'eux et commanda à sa fille d'en choisir un pour mary afin qu'il se battist contre l'autre." [97] This is a change from the text by Castillo Solórzano where the father is not such a just man; instead, in the Spanish version, Dom Manuel wants his daughter to marry Dom Juan.

Although Scarron eliminates all mythological allusions, he adds a literary allusion:

> Ils se virent souvent dans le mesme lieu et de la mesme façon qu'ils s'estoient veus la premiere fois et vinrent à s'aymer si fort que, sans répandre leur sang comme Pyrame et Tisbé, ils ne leur en deurent guere en tendresse impetueuse. [98]

Scarron makes a point of stating that this love did not end in tragedy. The reason is the striking difference in the parents. While in the story of Pyrame and Tisbé they opposed the marriage, as stated before, the father of Dorotée asked his daugther to make her own choice. Thus, justice is achieved.

The very last lines of the story again point to Scarron's ideas:

> Tout y alla bien de part et d'autre et mesme longtemps, ce qui est à considerer. [99]

This order which has been achieved is a lasting one, since it is based on all possible stabilizing factors: reason, authority, justice, and love. All other stories by Scarron ended simply in marriage. Nothing was said of the future, since it was in doubt. Here, all is certain. This conclusion also mirrors the conclusion of the *Roman comique,* which Scarron never wrote. The work would probably have proceeded from the harmony and justice achieved by Estoile and Destin to their final harmony with society through the approval of her father. Thus, Scarron sets forth that one must try to reconcile the different virtues and emotions into a lasting order based on reality.

---

[97] *Ibid.,* p. 794.
[98] *Ibid.,* p. 780.
[99] *Ibid.,* p. 794.

CONCLUSION

Paul Scarron's *Roman comique* contains four interpolated stories, three taken from Alonso de Castillo Solórzano and one from María de Zayas y Sotomayor. The French author changed the Spanish stories to make them fit, not only the tone but also the theme of the novel, which was inspired by Cervantes' *Don Quijote de la Mancha*.

The "Histoire de l'amante invisible" is the first of the four interpolated stories. Scarron realized that it was a romanesque tale expressing the same ideas as the heroic novels of the time. The French author, opposed to these ideas, ridiculed the hero, Dom Carlos, as well as the *précieux* manner used by Castillo Solórzano or that of any French novelist may have used in narrating the story. The fact that Ragotin tells the tale, and his resemblance to Dom Carlos adds to the satir eand links the story to the rest of the novel.

While the first interpolated story discussed an extreme type of emotion which Scarron considers inappropriate, the second interpolated story, "A trompeur, trompeur et demi" discusses the opposite extreme in "love" which is the lack of responsibility. Between both stories, Scarron includes the *récit* of Destin and Estoile. This middle ground between excessive idealization and lack of responsibility in love is what Scarron considers suitable, and offers it to the reader as an example of how things should be. Thus, the first part of the *Roman comique* is an organic whole since it discusses the diferent attitudes toward love.

The second interpolated story has also been considered by many critics as a model of how Scarron can improve on the Spanish original. The fact is that Scarron had not just one model but two for this tale, and took what he thought best from either one. They are the third interpolated story in *La garduña de Sevilla* (1642) and the second story in *Los alivios de Casandra* (1640).

Turning to the second half of the *Roman comique* published six years later, the main concern here is with justice. Love is seen only as an aspect of this justice. The *récit* of La Caverne, along with the two interpolated Spanish stories, one by María de Zayas and the other by Alonso de Castillo Solórzano, also make up an organic whole since all three deal with justice. La Caverne's story presents a lack of justice. "Le Juge de sa propre cause" presents an imperfect retributive justice, while "Les deux frères rivaux" deals with distributive justice or the harmony that is attained when all the parts are in their place, functioning properly.

In addition, all four stories further interact with the rest of the novel since they mirror the present action. This action is related to the action in Cervantes' masterpiece since the theme is similar, and Ragotin's adventures parallel those of the knight of la Mancha.

Thus, as opposed to most critics of the *Roman comique,* we conclude after careful examination of the way Scarron changes the Spanish tales to have them fit his novel, and taking into account that he had *Don Quijote de la Mancha* in mind when he began writing his novel, that the four interpolated stories are not extraneous to the novel but an integral part of it, since they underline the theme, parallel the plot, and mirror the action.

BIBLIOGRAPHY

Secondary Sources

ADAM, ANTOINE. *Histoire de la littérature française au XVIIe siècle.* Paris: Éditions Mondiales, 1962.

———, éd. *Romanciers du XVIIe siècle.* Paris: Bibliothèque de la Pléiade, 1962.

BALDENPERGER, F. "Les burlesques; Sorel, Furetière, Scarron," *RCC*, 21 (April 1, 1912), pp. 741-49.

BALDNER, RALPH W. "The Nouvelles Françaises of Segrais," *Modern Language Quarterly*, XVIII (1957).

BARDON, MAURICE. *"Don Quichotte" en France au XVIIe et au XVIIIe siècle.* Paris: Librairie Ancienne Honoré Champion, 1931.

BOURLAND, CAROLINE B. *The Short Story in Spain in the Seventeenth Century.* Portland, Maine: Southworth Press, 1927.

CADOREL, R. *Scarron et la nouvelle espagnole dans le Roman comique.* Aix-en-Provence: La Pensée Universitaire, 1960.

CAZEVANNE, JEAN. "Le Roman Hispano-Mauresque en France," *Revue de la littérature comparée*, V (1925).

CHANDLER, FRANK W. *Romances of Roguery.* New York: The Macmillan Company, 1899.

CHARDON, HENRI. *Scarron inconnu.* Paris: Champion, 1904.

COTARELO Y MORI, DON EMILIO, ed. *Colección selecta de antiguas novelas españolas*, Vol. III. Madrid: Librería de la Viuda de Rico, 1906.

CROOKS, ESTHER J. *The Influence of Cervantes in France in the Seventeenth Century.* Baltimore: Johns Hopkins Press, 1931.

DALLAS, DOROTHY FRANCES. *Le Roman français de 1660 à 1680.* Paris: Librairie Universitaire J. Gamber, 1932.

DEMOGEOT, J. *Histoire des littératures étrangères. Littératures méridionales: Italie-Espagne.* Paris: Librairie Hachette, 1892.

ENGSTROM, ALFRED G. *The French Artistic Short Story Before Maupassant.* Chapel Hill: 1941.

FERNÁNDEZ NAVARRETE, E. "Bosquejo histórico sobre la Novela" in *B.A.E.*, Vol. XXXIII. Madrid: Imprenta de los sucesores de Hernando, 1914.

HAINSWORTH, G. *Les "Novelas Ejemplares" de Cervantes en France au XVIIe siècle.* Paris: Librairie Ancienne Honoré Champion, 1933.

———. "New details on the *Nouvelles* of Scarron and Boisrobert," *Bulletin Hispanique*, 49 (1947).

HASSELMAN, JULES, éd. *Les Conteurs français du XVIe siècle.* Paris: Librairie Larousse, 1945.
LANCASTER, HENRY CARRINGTON. *A History of French Dramatic Literature in the Seventeenth Century,* Vols. III and IV. Baltimore: Johns Hopkins Press, 1936.
LANSON, GUSTAVE. "Études sur les rapports de la littérature française et de la littérature espagnole au XVIIe siècle (1600-1660)," *R.H.L.F.,* III (1896).
LE BRETON, ANDRÉ. *Le roman au XVIIe siècle.* Paris: Librairie Hachette, 1890.
LOUANDRE, CHARLES. "Les conteurs français au XVIIe siècle,"*Revue des Deux Mondes,* 44 (1874).
MAGENDIE, MAURICE. *Le roman français au XVIIe siècle de l'Astrée au Grand Cyrus.* Paris: E. Droz, 1932.
MAGNE, ÉMILE. *Le Plaisant Abbé de Boisrobert.* Paris: Mercure de France, 1909.
———. *Scarron et son milieu.* Paris: Émile Paul frères, 1924.
MALKIEWICZ. "Un remaniement de la Vie est Songe," *Revue de littérature comparée,* XIX (1939).
MARTINENCHE, E. *La Comedia espagnole en France de Hardy à Racine.* Paris: Hachette et Cie, 1900.
MENÉNDEZ Y PELAYO, M. *Orígenes de la Novela,* Vol. 2. Madrid: Bailly-Ballière é Hijos, 1907.
MORILLOT, PAUL. *Le Roman en France depuis 1610 jusqu'à nos jours, lectures et esquisses.* Paris: G. Masson, 1892.
———. *Scarron et le genre burlesque.* Paris: Lecène et H. Oudin, 1888.
PLACE, EDWIN. *Bosquejo histórico de la novela corta y el cuento durante el Siglo de Oro.* Madrid: Victoriano Suárez, editor, 1926.
———. "María de Zayas, an outstanding woman short-story writer of Seventeenth Century Spain," *University of Colorado Studies,* XIII (June, 1923).
PUIBUSQUE, ADOLPHE DE. *Histoire comparée des littératures espagnole et française.* Paris: Chez G. A. Dentu, 1843.
RATNER, MOSES. *Theory and Criticism of the Novel in France from L'Astrée to 1750.* New York: De Palma Printing Co., 1938.
RAYNAL, MARIE ALINE. *La Nouvelle française de Segrais à Mme de La Fayette.* Paris: Librairie Picart, 1926.
REYNIER, GUSTAVE. *Le Roman réaliste au XVIIe siècle.* Paris: Librairie Hachette, 1914.
RUNDLE, J. U. "The Sources of Dryden's Comic Plot in *The Assignation,*" *Modern Philology,* XLV (1947-1948).
SAINTSBURY, GEORGE. *A History of the French Novel.* London: Macmillan and Co., 1917-1919.
SAÍNZ DE ROBLES, FEDERICO CARLOS, ed. *Cuentos viejos de la vieja España.* Madrid: Aguilar, 1949.
SALCEDO RUIZ, ÁNGEL. *La Literatura española.* Madrid: Editorial Calleja, 1916.
SCARRON, PAUL. *Le Roman comique,* Félix Guirand and André V. Pierre, eds. Paris: Librairie Larousse, 1935.
SCHWEITZER, JEROME. "George de Scudéry's *Almahide,*" *Johns Hopkins Studies in Romance Literatures and Languages,* XXXIV (1939).
SIMON, ERNEST. "The Function of the Spanish Stories in Scarron's *Roman comique,*" *L'Esprit Créateur,* III (Fall, 1963).

SYLVANIA, LENA E. *Doña María de Zayas y Sotomayor: A Contribution to the Study of her Works.* New York: Columbia U. Press, 1922.
TIPPING, WESSIE M. *Jean Regnauld de Segrais: L'homme et son œuvre.* Paris: Les éditions Internationales, 1933.
TUCKER, J. E. "The Earliest English Translations of Scarron's *nouvelles*," *Revue de la Littérature comparée,* XXIV (1950).
VOGLER, FREDERICK W. *Vital d'Audiguier and the Early Seventeenth Century French Novel.* Chapel Hill: U. of North Carolina Press, 1964.

PRIMARY SOURCES

BOISROBERT, FRANÇOIS LE METEL DE. *La Belle invisible ou la constance esprouvvée.* Paris: Guillaume de Luyne, 1656.
―――. *La Jalouse d'elle-mesme.* Paris: Augustin Courbé, 1659.
CALDERÓN DE LA BARCA, PEDRO. *La dama duende* in *comedias de capa y espada,* Vol. 2. Madrid: Espasa-Calpe, 1954.
―――. *Mañanas de Abril y Mayo* in *Colección de las piezas dramáticas de los autores españoles.* Madrid: Imprenta de D. A. Fernández, 1826.
CASTILLO SOLÓRZANO, ALONSO DE. *Los alivios de Casandra.* Barcelona: Emprenta de Jayme Romeu, 1640.
―――. *La garduña de Sevilla y anzuelo de las bolsas.* Madrid: Ediciones de "La Lectura," 1922.
CERVANTES, MIGUEL, DE. *Don Quijote de la Mancha.* Martín de Riquer, ed. Barcelona: Editorial Juventud, S. A., 1967.
―――. *Novelas ejemplares.* Buenos Aires: Editorial Sopena, Argentina, S. A., 1962.
FURETIÈRE, ANTOINE. *Le Roman bourgeois,* in *Romanciers du XVIIe siècle.* Paris: Bibliothèque de la Pléiade, 1962.
HUET, PIERRE DANIEL. *De l'origine des romans* in *Œuvres* by Marie Madeleine comtesse de La Fayette. Paris: Garnier frères, 1864.
LA FAYETTE, MARIE MADELEINE COMTESSE DE. *La Princesse de Clèves,* in *Romanciers du XVIIe siècle.* Paris: Bibliothèque de la Pléiade, 1962.
OUVILLE, ANTOINE LE METEL SIEUR D'. *Aimer sans sçavoir qui.* Paris: Cardin Besogne, 1647.
―――. *Histoire et aventures de Doña Rufine.* La Haye: Chez A. Van Dole, 1743.
OTWAY, THOMAS. *The Atheist,* in *The Works of Thomas Otway,* J. C. Ghosh, ed. Oxford: Clarendon Press, 1932.
SCARRON, PAUL. *Roman comique* in *Romanciers du XVIIe siècle.* Paris: Bibibliothèque de la Pléiade, 1962.
SOREL, CHARLES. *La Bibliothèque française,* Myron L. Kocher, ed. Chapel Hill: 1965.
TALLEMANT DES REAUX, GÉDÉON. *Historiettes,* Antoine, éd. Paris: Librairie Gallimard, 1960.
TIRSO DE MOLINA. *La Celosa de sí misma,* in *Obras dramáticas completas,* Blanca de los Ríos, ed. Madrid: Aguilar, S. A., 1952.
URFÉE, HONORÉ D'. *L'Astrée.* Paris: Librairie Larousse, 1935.
ZAYAS Y SOTOMAYOR, DOÑA MARÍA DE. *Novelas amorosas y ejemplares.* Madrid: Aldus, 1948.

www.ingramcontent.com/pod-product-compliance
Lightning Source LLC
Chambersburg PA
CBHW020418230426
43663CB00007BA/1221